MOORINGS IN A WORLD ADRIFT

Answers for Christians Who Dare to Ask Why

B. CLAYTON BELL, SR.

 HarperSanFrancisco
A Division of HarperCollins*Publishers*

MOORINGS IN A WORLD ADRIFT: *Answers for Christians Who Dare to Ask Why*. Copyright © 1990 by Benjamin Clayton Bell, Sr. All rights reserved. Printed in the United States of America. No part of this book may be used or reproduced in any manner whatsoever without written permission except in the case of brief quotations embodied in critical articles and reviews. For information address HarperCollins Publishers, 10 East 53rd Street, New York, NY 10022.

FIRST EDITION

Library of Congress Cataloging-in-Publication Data
Bell, B. Clayton.
    Moorings in a world adrift/B. Clayton Bell, Sr.—1st
ad.
      p.   cm.
    ISBN 0–06–252024–5
    1. Apologetics—20th century. 2. Christian life—Presbyterian authors. I. Title.
    BT1102.B34 1990
    230—dc20   89-40632
                                          CIP

90 91 92 93 94 RRD 10 9 8 7 6 5 4 3 2 1

This edition is printed on acid-free paper that meets the American National Standards Institute Z39.48 Standard.

Seest thou another man shipwrecked? Look well to thy moorings!

—JOHN TRAPP, SIXTEENTH CENTURY

TABLE OF CONTENTS

ACKNOWLEDGMENTS

Special thanks are due to two people: to Austin Watson, a constant encourager, who keeps urging me to put material in print, and to Ves Box, who kept pushing me to put the Apostles' Creed sermons in book form, and then gave a valuable critique of my first draft. Thanks, dear friends. Your encouragement prodded me beyond my natural instincts.

And there are others to whom thanks are also due, for without them there would be no book.

My thanks to Jewell Smith for her diligent and efficient services as my sermon transcriber.

Thanks to Finley Ewing, a dear and generous friend, who read the first draft and whose enthusiasm gave me more encouragement than I deserved.

Thanks to Ernestine Van Buren, author, teacher, and grammarian, whose cogent comments and editorial honesty I will always appreciate.

Thanks to Ralph Gaden, who encouraged me more than he will ever know, when he told me what it meant to him when he inadvertently picked up the rough draft at Finley's Carmel house and read it through.

Thanks to my sister Ruth for the quotation from John Trapp.

Thanks to my secretary, Helen Bostick, across whose desk came a multitude of details that she handled for me so that I had the time to devote to this book.

But to my precious wife, Peggy, I give greatest thanks, for her constant encouragement, for being a friendly critic, for her daily support, and for her everlasting "Clayton, make it practical!" Thank the Lord for such a wonderful helper!

When asked by a student in class what should be the preacher's policy in the use of commentaries, sermons, and other material when preparing one's own sermon, my homiletics professor at Columbia Seminary said, "Graze where you want to, but give your own milk."

To innumerable pastures of learning and print where I have grazed, my deepest thanks. I have given credit where I am aware of the source. But for the milk of insight contained in these pages, I alone, for credit or blame, take responsibility.

And to God alone be all the glory and the praise!

INTRODUCTION

You are a theologian.

"Wait a minute!" you reply. "I'm no theologian. I've never studied in a seminary. And I get epistles confused with Apostles. You're really pushing credibility to call me a theologian."

But I didn't say you were a good theologian. Some theologians are good theologians and some are poor. Do you think about God? Do you wonder about the meaning of life, why you are here? Do you make decisions based on whether you think human beings can be trusted? If so, you are a theologian.

"Aren't you using the word *theologian* a little loosely?" you say. "After all, there are people who have been to seminary, have other advanced degrees, study the Bible seriously, have read many volumes of theology, and maybe have even written some of those volumes. Wouldn't they have the right to feel slighted by your calling me a theologian? After all, I drive a car but I'm no mechanic. I know how to flip a light switch, but I'm no electrician."

Okay, you are technically right. Maybe you're not a theologian in the exact sense. But God isn't an organized package of nuts, bolts, and sheet metal, and he's not a systematic compilation of wires. If God is a Being with whom you relate on a personal basis, then you don't leave this personal relationship to others to handle. And if you think God isn't a Being with whom you relate on a personal basis, then you have made a theological decision. You may not be a mechanic, but if you decide to drive a car you have made a decision about mechanics. You may not be an electrician, but if you decide to have your house wired for electricity, you have made a decision about electricity. Even if you decide not to drive or use electricity, if they are available otions, then you have made a decision involving mechanics and electricity. In that sense, then, you make theological decisions every day.

So wouldn't it be a good idea to make intelligent decisions, based on at least the fundamental elements of theology?

Many people seem to think that "theology" is for preachers and other impractical people. But theology is the most important field of knowledge you can investigate. It is nothing more or less than what you believe about God and how you are to live in response to him. If there is a God, and if human beings must at some point stand before him and give an accounting of their lives, then it is pretty important to know what to expect.

In 1984 I preached a series of sermons on the Apostles' Creed to my congregation at Highland Park Presbyterian Church in Dallas, Texas. The Apostles' Creed is a statement of faith that is used by the Roman Catholic church and by many Protestant churches. It is not a complete summary of the Christian faith, but it states in simple language what we Christians believe about God, Jesus, the Holy Spirit, the church, forgiveness, and eternal life. Indications are that it was used early in church history in question form to quiz converts as to their faith.

The people of my congregation were enthusiastic in their appreciation of the series, and some suggested that I put the series into book form.

But sermons in book form can be pretty dull stuff. I have no desire to add to their number. So what lies ahead bears little resemblance to the sermons originally preached. There is, however, a crying need for Christians, whether new converts or longtime pew-sitters, to face life and make decisions with an understanding of the basics of the faith to which Christians are committed.

Not only is it important for Christians to order their own lives theologically, *but if the truth of biblical faith is really true,* then it is incumbent upon believers to lovingly persuade the drifting world to anchor at these same moorings.

THE APOSTLES' CREED

I believe in God the Father Almighty, maker of
    heaven and earth;
And in Jesus Christ his only Son our Lord;
    who was conceived by the Holy Ghost;
    born of the Virgin Mary;
    suffered under Pontius Pilate;
    was crucified, dead and buried.
    He descended into Hell;
    the third day He rose again from the dead;
    He ascended into heaven;
    and sitteth on the right hand of God the
        Father Almighty;
    from thence He shall come to judge the quick
        and the dead.
I believe in the Holy Ghost;
    the holy catholic church,
    the communion of saints,
    the forgiveness of sins,
    the resurrection of the body,
    and the life everlasting.

AMEN!

START HERE

Faith: You Can't Live Without It!

The phone call caught me by surprise.

"Clayton, would you and Peggy be willing to come to our house for supper Friday night—and be prepared to work?"

"Thanks for the invitation, Bob. I'll check with Peggy, but I think we can. What's up?"

Thus began a delightful string of evenings with four young, attractive couples who dared to be honest about their doubts. I say "delightful" because genuine honesty is hard to come by, especially for a minister. The face we most often meet is the religious mask intended to impress the clergyperson with how good the wearer is. To admit doubt is tantamount to high treason of the soul. To deal with people honestly, to hear and respond to their genuine concerns, to wrestle with them about their doubts, is a real delight.

The conversations of those evenings have haunted my memory over the years. I buried one of the wives in that octet, and one couple divorced after we left that pastorate. I have not kept in touch with the other two couples. But that at least some of the group were helped toward greater faith, and that this writer was helped, is certain.

We had eaten a delicious supper and were seated in chairs and on cushions on the living room floor when the work started. Bob started the conversation for the group.

"Clayton, we were all raised in this church, and all our lives we have been told there is a God, that Jesus Christ is his Son, that he was born of a virgin, and that he rose from the dead. And now we hear you saying the same thing and it doesn't seem reasonable. It seems to me that you and the church are asking us to believe all of this on blind faith."

My mind immediately began to marshal all of the theological arguments I had learned in seminary about the existence of God. The "teleological argument," the "ontological argument," and the "cosmological argument" were rusty weapons in the closet of my mind. But I had learned a little about theological debate in my thirteen years as a minister, and that was why those weapons were rusting back in a dark corner of my mind: I had never found them to work.

"Bob," I asked, "what is the logical alternative to saying, 'I believe in God'?"

There was a moment of silence as his lawyer's mind thought through that one before he replied, "I guess it would be, 'I don't believe there is a God.' "

"May I rephrase that to say, 'I believe there is no God'?" I asked.

Again he paused a moment, and said, "Yes, that's acceptable."

"If 'I believe there is no God' is the logical alternative to 'I believe in God,' does it take any more blind faith to 'believe in God' than it does to 'believe there is no God'? Both of those statements are statements of faith, are they not? We cannot prove that there is a God or that there is no God; ultimately, it takes a leap of faith to end up on either side."

This is no capitulation to anti-intellectualism. There is much intelligent reasoning that can be brought to bear on the side of believing in God, and in Jesus Christ as the Son of God and the Savior of humanity. But the plain fact is that both the theist and the atheist are people of faith. Both Madalyn Murray O'Hair and Billy Graham use the same tools. They just happen to be digging in different mines.

And therein lies the crux of faith. It is not the capacity of faith, but rather the object of faith, that determines the ultimate outcome of life and eternity.

As a young person I used to sing a chorus in youth meetings that went

Only believe, only believe,
All things are possible, only believe.

That chorus glorified the capacity of faith. *But faith in what?*

I had a professor in seminary who said that faith is to the soul what swallowing is to the body—and the health of the body is largely dependent on what is swallowed.

And that is the purpose of the Apostles' Creed: to provide the minimum daily requirement that the soul must swallow to be healthy.

The Apostles' Creed is a statement of faith used by the early church as a concise declaration of what Christians believe. The earliest example of the Latin text of the Apostles' Creed in its modern form dates from about the eighth century A.D. But similar statements of faith can be traced all the way back to the second century A.D.

The New Testament itself contains some brief summaries of faith, such as Paul's statement in 1 Corinthians 15:3–5: "For what I received I passed on to you as of first importance: that Christ died for our sins according to the Scriptures, that He was buried, that He was raised on the third day according to the Scriptures, and that He appeared to Peter, and then to the Twelve."

With this Paul states that he is transmitting to his readers a body of truth that he himself received.

But Paul also indicates a priority of things to be believed: "What I received I passed on to you as of *first importance.*" There are some doctrines in the Christian faith that are more foundational than others. They represent the very essence of Christianity, and the absence of such essentials means the reality is not present.

The Apostles' Creed opens with a simple assertion: "I believe." Faith is the place where all of life's experiences begin. We call a baby's faith "instinct," for instinctively the newborn infant nuzzles her mother's breast, knowing that nourishment is to be found there. It is by instinct that a baby feels the comfort and security of her mother's arms and quietly sleeps. It is by instinct that a baby cries as a way of communicating that something is wrong and calls for someone to respond to her need.

Every person is born into this world with the ability to believe. It is negative experience that tends to make unbelievers out of believers. Experience sometimes makes cynics out of people who have goodwill. A baby instinctively turns to her mother's breast for food, but some mothers don't have milk, or mother's milk doesn't agree with the baby, so then it's the bottle. But in some places there are no bottles.

Or a toddler reaches out a hand for support, only to have his hand dropped.

Or a young person takes an adult at his word, and then bitterly discovers that not all adults keep their word.

Nevertheless, the Biblical assumption is that we all have a capacity for faith and that unless that faith has been tampered with by someone else or Someone else, that capacity for faith is going to be directed toward God. Anything else is called unbelief.

So, the Bible does not try to prove the existence of God. The writers of the Scriptures assume that God *is,* that God is approachable, and that God enters into meaningful relationships with people.

So does the Apostles' Creed. It starts with the simple assumption of one's capacity for faith, and asserts that the object of faith is God.

When I was a little boy of three or four, I was with my parents, who were medical missionaries in China. I asked my father one day, "What is faith?" "Son," he replied, "wait until this afternoon and I will show you."

We were living in a city about 150 miles north of Shanghai, in North Kiangsu Province. The summers were hot and humid, and air-conditioning was not in existence. As partial relief from the oppressive heat, my father had Chinese workmen construct a swimming pool in our side yard. Now, lest the reader become disillusioned with the austere lifestyle of missionaries, let me hasten to add that this pool was nothing more than a concrete box about eight feet wide and twelve feet long, and maybe five feet deep at its deepest point. But to a little boy it looked olympic-sized. When my father returned from the hospital that afternoon, we put on our swim suits and headed to the pool. I had not yet learned to swim, and after my father got in the pool at its deepest point, he turned to me, held out his hands and said, "Jump." Without a moment's hesitation, I jumped into his waiting hands. Then, lifting me out of the water and setting me down on the pool's edge, he said, "Son, that is faith. I told you to jump, you believed I would catch you, so you obeyed my word. And faith in God is not just believing he exists, but doing what he says because you believe he will keep his promises."

When I think of the wisdom of a godly father in teaching his small son the meaning of faith, I can't help but contrast that with a story I once heard and hope is not true. A father put his son up on a high fence, told him to jump, and when the boy obeyed, the father stepped back and let the boy take a hard fall on the ground. As the boy got up crying, the father said, "Now let that be a lesson to you never to trust anybody."

Yet all of us, even the most disillusioned, go through life exercising faith every day. We exercise faith in business relationships. If we can't take a person's word for a deal, we sign a document. We still use faith, though it is transferred from the spoken word to the written word on the document. If we don't trust the written agreement between the other person and ourselves, then we hire lawyers to draw up the documents, and after signatures are witnessed by the appropriate number of witnesses, we exercise faith in lawyers, legal documents and witnesses. And we exercise faith especially in the legal system to make the whole arrangement work.

For a number of years, I have wanted to see the Oberammergau Passion Play in Germany. When I heard that a special 350th-anniversary performance would be presented during the summer of 1984, I made plans to lead a tour that would include the play. When planning such a tour, one always seeks a reputable travel agency and depends upon it to make arrangements for travel, housing, special tours, performance tickets, and local transportation. And when tourists sign up for such a trip, they are taking the word of the tour conductor who in turn trusts the agency. So when fifty-four people signed up for the trip, they did so on the assumption that they would go to the places and do the things advertised for the tour.

However, I had heard that for the 1980 season in Oberammergau, counterfeit tickets had, in some instances, been issued and people arrived in the town only to find that their tickets were not valid. So I made several inquiries of my travel agent, expressed my apprehensions, and received multiple reassurances from him that his ticket source was fully reliable.

With all of his reassurance, I still felt some apprehension which was not fully relieved until we arrived in Oberammergau on the appointed day and found empty seats that matched our ticket stubs. The travel agent trusted his tour agency sources; I trusted the travel agent; fifty-four people took my word; and interconnecting all of these arrangements and relationships was a continuous network of faith in planes, pilots, navigational equipment, travel documents, chefs, and so on. Faith made that trip possible. And it makes every day of life possible, because one cannot live and move on without it. It is what keeps the world functioning.

But why the use of the first person singular, "I?" Didn't Jesus teach his disciples to pray, "Our Father, who art in heaven . . . ?" Isn't there something immodestly selfish about starting off the Creed with "*I* believe . . . ?"

If one never progressed beyond saying "I" and "my," the answer would be an unequivocal 'yes.' But a baby has to be able to know the "I" of self-identity before it can affirm the "we" of family life. The writers of the Creed affirmed what is clearly stated in the New Testament, that faith is at first intensely personal before it is communal. When we are *in* the family, then life is a family affair. But getting into the family is a very personal and individual matter. The record indicates that Jesus called people individually to be his disciples, and then taught them to pray "*Our* Father . . . ."

But perhaps what we need to keep in mind here is the matter of balance. A baby is not the result of self generation, but of the cooperation of father and mother. He is an individual who belongs to a family. His emotional and social health involve the balance of understanding his personal identity as a community member, while still maintaining his sense of individuality in the community.

"I believe" and "Our Father" are the subjective and the objective sides of faith, and those statements are also the private and the communal side of our relationships. We have a capacity for faith which we exercise every day, and God has given us a community of faith to help us focus faith on eternal ground that never gives way in the storms of life.

We believe. We believe because we have been born with that ability. Yet, when it comes to focusing on faith, we may be like the father whose son was possessed by a demon (Mark 9:17–24). When he met Jesus, he pled, "If you can do anything, take pity on us and help us." Jesus responded, "If you can? Everything is possible for him who believes." And the boy's father immediately responded, "I do believe; help me overcome my unbelief."

And we, too, believe. But experience sometimes disillusions us, the Enemy diverts our attention from the only trustworthy object of faith, and we, like that father, cry out, "Lord, I do believe; help me overcome the unbelief that has crept into my soul."

We can't live a day without faith. And, depending upon where we place our faith, with faith we can live forever.

Chapter 1

THE GOD WHO IS BIG ENOUGH FOR LIFE

"I Believe in God the Father Almighty, Maker of Heaven and Earth."

Why do some people commit suicide?

There is probably a different answer for every suicide. An adult whose business has failed, or one whose spouse has deserted him, or one who has been told she has an incurable disease, may decide to end it all.

A recent phenomenon on the American sociological scene is the marked rise of teenage suicide. Several years ago in a Houston suburb, shortly afterward in a North Dallas suburb, and more recently in an eastern town, there has been a spate of teenage suicides. Anytime a person takes his or her own life, those who knew the person ask why. This is especially true when a teenager commits suicide. Why would a young person who still has all the prospects of life ahead snuff out his or her own existence?

Those of us who counsel people threatening to take their lives, or who deal with families shattered by suicide, know there is no simple answer to that question. For some people it is a matter of an emotional or a body chemistry imbalance that leads to an ultimately fatal depression. For those who take their own lives, suicide seems a sensible alternative to the future. Whatever is the motivating cause behind suicide there is this one kernel of truth in their experience; from their perspective, suicide seems a better alternative than living in the future.

Some months ago I was astonished to see on television news a crowd of men marching through the streets of Teheran pounding themselves on their foreheads and scalps until their heads were bloody masses and blood streamed down their faces, soaking their shirts. In this way they sought to demonstrate their loyalty to Allah and their preparedness to give their lives in destroying the hated foreigners and the hated disbelievers, especially Americans. They were Shiite Muslims vowing their loyalty to the Jihad, the holy war.

What do teen suicides and Iranian fanatics have in common? Each presupposes a view of God. What people believe about God determines what they believe about themselves. What they believe about God also determines their outlook on the world and the other people in it. Some give up on God; their alternative, then, is to end their lives. Others, fervently believing in God, think the best way—God's way—is "to destroy the accursed infidels" and to be prepared to give their lives in the process.

The prophet Isaiah says

"To whom will you compare me? Or who is my equal?" says the Holy One. Lift up your eyes and look to the heavens; who created all these? He who brings out the starry host one by one, and calls them each by name. Because of His great power and mighty strength, not one of them is missing.

Why do you say, O Jacob, and complain, O Israel, "My way is hidden from the Lord; my cause is disregarded by my God"? Do you not know? Have you not heard? The Lord is the everlasting God, the Creator of the ends of the earth. He will not grow tired or weary, and his understanding no one can fathom. He gives strength to the weary and increases the power of the weak. Even youths grow tired and weary, and young men stumble and fall; but those who hope in the Lord will renew their strength. They will soar on wings like eagles; they will run and not grow weary, they will walk and not be faint. (Isa. 40:25–31)

The true God is unequaled, is the Creator of all things, is fully aware of the circumstances of his children, is untiring in his care for his creatures, and gives strength to those who hope in him. God is big enough for all of life and every circumstance of life. This is the God in whom the creed affirms faith.

Toward the end of my first year in college I felt that God wanted me in the ministry. I had been raised in a godly home with a healthy, positive Christian atmosphere. The peer pressure of my parents' generation measured piety, at least in part, by the pleasures that were prohibited. Alcohol and tobacco were strict taboos. Mother used to play bridge, but when she and Dad went to China as missionaries, she gave it up because of the attitude of other missionaries toward the use of cards. Rook, however, was somehow exempt from the onus of other card games, so mother was the Rook shark of the mission compound. Movies, dancing (round, not square), and all nonreligious Sunday activities were verboten. In spite of this excessive limitation of pleasurable activities, life was very full and home life was fun.

But with the inner sense of call to the ministry, I was faced with a crisis: what would I preach? I believed the Gospel, which I would preach, but the parish preacher is called upon to do more than convert people every Sunday. What would be the broader scope of my preaching? What would be its moral and ethical dimensions?

During the summer months I stayed in school to take a course in Greek. I spent a great deal of time with Burt Harding, a graduate student, who shared with me a love for tennis. Between sets, as we took a breather, I discussed my dilemma with Burt. "Burt, I know God has called me to be a minister, but when I think about the broader dimensions of preaching, I become frustrated. I believe that Jesus is the Son of God and my Savior, and I don't drink, smoke, play cards, dance, or go to movies; but the idea of preaching that to people isn't a goal to which I want to give my life."

"Clayton," Burt replied, "have you read J. B. Phillips's book *Your God Is Too Small!*" I hadn't, so the next day he presented me with a copy. From the vantage point of years later, I now realize it was that book which freed me to go into the ministry. God used that book to impress upon me two things. First, God's will is not to be confused with the cultural taboos often promulgated by well-meaning Christian people. Second, God is as big as the outpouring of his love and will revealed in Jesus Christ, and the way to know him is to know his whole written Word through the indwelling power and presence of the Holy Spirit.

What kind of God is big enough for our lives? To answer that question we must look at the component parts of life. First, is God big enough to give life meaning?

The very foundation of our own existence is our own sense of who we are and why we are here. What is the purpose for our lives? What is the purpose behind history, which is simply the composite story of the lives of people living through the ages? How did we get here? Are we merely the result of the unions of our mothers and fathers? Are we meaningless nonentities on the way to meaninglessness? Are we here by accident? Or is there a divine cause and purpose behind our existence?

Another component of life involves the various events which, when taken together, make up the course of human history. Is God bigger than the events of life, individually or taken together? The things that happen to us and the things we see happening around us raise all kinds of questions about existence and purpose and duty. We see retarded children and wonder about the cause. Is God big enough to deal with our own questions about the tragedies and heartaches of life? Accidents, disease, suffering in a wide variety of forms, the injustice and inequity that we see in our own lives and in our communities and the world: all of these raise questions. The question is, Is God big enough to deal with them? Is the God we worship bigger than history?

After the train of events has run its course, we come inevitably to the last chapter, which is death. Or is it the last chapter? Is God bigger than death? Is there more to life than existence?

The evidence for the existence of God is substantial, in fact, overwhelming. But in the final analysis, there can be no conviction about God, be it his existence or nonexistence, without a leap of faith. Having dealt with that in the opening chapter, I will assume in this chapter that the reader is a believer. The more appropriate question before us now is, In what kind of God do we believe? It is not enough to say that we believe in God, for all kinds of excesses and cruelties are committed by human beings in the name of "God."

The Apostles' Creed starts with the affirmation "I believe in God the Father." The word *father* describes God both in his relationships and in his disposition. In regard to his relationships, he is the originator. He is the One who started our existence. But in this particular context in the Apostles' Creed, it has special reference to his relationship to the Son, Jesus Christ. As it describes the disposition of the Father, that word, *father,* describes his compassion, his love, his caring, his support of his family. The psalmist wrote, "As a father has compassion on his children, so the Lord has compassion on those who fear him; for he knows how we are formed, he remembers that we are dust." (Ps. 103:13–14). Numerous other passages in both the Old and New Testaments describe God as a Father who cares, who supports, who sometimes disciplines (but always disciplines with a constructive end in mind), and who leads his children to what is best for them.

But is the word *father* a positive word to use of God, in an age when so few people seem to have positive images of their earthly fathers? Your attitude toward God as Father is inevitably colored by your attitude toward your own earthly father. If your earthly father was strong, kind, supportive, and encouraging, then it is easier for you to accept God as Father than it is for those whose fathers were mean, abusive, neglectful, or surly.

A friend recently told me that his father never told him he was proud of him. This friend still longed for his father to affirm him. He knew that his father loved him, but he was never sure that his father was pleased with him. Consequently he found it easy to believe that God loved him, but it was very hard for him to feel that he was acceptable to God, that God was pleased with him.

But I have found in my counseling that many of those whose fathers were weak or abusive or otherwise disappointing still have a concept of "father" to which they sense their own earthly fathers do not meet. The word *father* carries with it its own intuitively understood definition. When we affirm our faith in God the Father, we are saying that God more than fulfills that definition. He is supportive; he loves; he cares what happens.

But if that is all that God is, then no matter how kindly his disposition, how good his intentions, he still may be impotent in the face of reality. An accident is a reality, cancer is a reality, a heart attack is a reality, depression is a reality, and death is very real and very final. Is God bigger than these?

The Apostles' Creed defines the disposition of God with the word *father*, but expands the potential of that disposition with the word *almighty*. If God is only good, and not all-powerful, then his disposition toward us may be kindly; but he may not have the power to make sure that good happens to us. The word *almighty* comes from a Greek word, *pantocrator*, which more accurately should be rendered as "all-ruling" or "all-controlling." It connotes the act of governing in past, present, and future. Nothing is out of his control. It means that the God who is described as almighty is *the God who is in control of history:* yours, mine, and the world's. Nothing is beyond his power. To be sure, that raises questions about some of the events we witness and some of the catastrophes we observe. We draw back and wonder, How could God allow that? Even if we say that God did not direct some tragedy, if he is all-powerful, by implication he could have stopped it, we think. Why did he not? It takes faith to believe that the God who is almighty is also our Father, and has promised, as Paul says, "All things work together for good for those who love Him" (Rom.)8:28 (KJV).

To say we "believe in God the Father almighty" may not answer all of our questions. There are many questions that the finite mind can ask that can be answered only from the perspective of infinity. But it gives us a point of reference to solve the dilemmas and problems of suffering and pain and hurt and tragedy. If we can say, "I believe in God the Father almighty," then we should not choke on anything else in the Apostles' Creed. The reason for this truth is that this statement of the power and personality of God provides us with the philosophical and theological foundation for everything else we affirm.

We declare that we "believe in God the Father almighty," and go on to say that he is the "maker of heaven and earth." Here we move into the question of creation, the who and the how. It is beyond the scope of this chapter to solve the controversy surrounding creation and evolution, but we can affirm that God is Creator.

Among those who believe that God is behind creation, there are some who believe that God created the world in six twenty-four-hour days; and there are others who believe that God created the world in six eras of time that are referred to as days. Their example is

the mother who says to her teenage daughter, "Back in my day
. . ." She is not talking about a twenty-four-hour period, but about
a period of her history.

The theory of evolution was not original with Darwin. It goes
back to the sixth century B.C., when two Greek philosophers,
Thales and Anaximander, propounded similar theories. Evolution
is simply a theory that resulted from people observing the universe
and trying to explain how it came into existence and how differences
came to be among the species.

But *the Bible is very clear that "in the beginning God created the heavens
and the earth."* The world is God's masterpiece. The sun and the
heavens declare the glory of God, and the skies proclaim his handi-
work. Paul, in Romans 1:20, writes, "For since the creation of the
world, God's invisible qualities, His eternal power and divine nature
have been clearly seen, being understood from what has been
made." The issue of great importance for us is the question, Is God
behind why we are here and where we are going?

A tragedy of modern education is that the theory of evolution is
taught as scientific fact, which is untrue. Several generations have
grown up believing that they are nothing more than a higher form
of vertebrate with no purpose for their existence, rather than knowing they are "made a little lower than the angels" and are part of the
marvelous plan of a loving Father. Because we must keep church
and state separate, public schooling cannot include biblical insights
into God's part in his creation. We are here because he is our
Creator.

Whether we believe God is behind a process that lasted millions of
years, or whether we believe that he created the world in six literal
twenty-four-hour days is, to some extent, beside the point *if* we
believe that God is behind the process.

One summer on family vacation in Colorado we drove to Lake
City, where we went into a quaint little jewelry store. In addition to
the handmade jewelry and other handicrafts displayed in glass
counters, my eye was caught by something hanging on the wall. It
was not a painting nor a sculpture. It was something like a plaque,
except mounted on the plaque was the facade of a miniature house,

which extended out in relief approximately four inches. The exquisite detail with which it was made and the care with which the artist had worked made it a perfect delight to see. Because woodworking is a hobby of mine, I was particularly enthralled with the careful, meticulous detail of the craft of the artisan. Another of this same artist's exhibits was nearly four feet long and included the facades of a variety of Old West storefronts. As I looked at this piece, I thought what a gifted, creative artist it was who had done the work. No matter how long it might have taken the artist to do the work, I was impressed. If he or she had done it in a matter of a few hours, I would would have been terribly impressed. I didn't inquire, so I never knew.

The next day I was floating down the Rio Grande River on a rubber raft. As I was looking at the rugged peaks and the bluffs of the San Juan Mountains, I saw the folds and the rocks and thought to myself, What a great God he is who created all of this. I wonder how long it took him? Maybe it took millions of years, but maybe he did it in six twenty-four-hour days. As I thought about that, my mind returned to my admiration of the exquisite detail of the artist who had constructed the three-dimensional wall plaques I had seen the day before. Could it be that our God is such a great artist that this world which he has put here and with which he took such great care and through which he exhibits such great power was created in a matter of hours rather than millions of years? I do not know. That thought, however, created within me a great sense of awe and wonder that that is the kind of God we worship. *He indeed is a God who is big enough for life.*

But then a question entered my mind: If God did create the world in six days, was it not a dirty trick to make it look like five hundred million years? Wouldn't it be dishonest for God to fool us like that? As I considered my own question, the answer came to me, No, not really. If God did make it in six days, then what looks like five hundred million years is merely the measure of our lack of belief in a God who is big enough to tackle such a job and pull it off.

My wife gave me an amazing watch one Christmas. It had a dial and hands that told the time. It also had a digital readout. These could be set differently to mark different time zones, if need be, which was helpful when making phone calls or when traveling. The digital time could even be set to military time, giving time in twenty-four hour segments rather than two twelve-hour segments. It had two alarms plus a stopwatch. It was an amazing watch.

On a recent trip to Singapore I bought another watch that had five alarms, a stopwatch, a timer, and could be set to register time in twenty-three time zones. And it cost one-tenth of what my wife paid for the first watch.

Now, if I had come from a nontechnical society and had seen these watches, and if someone had explained to me all that they would do, what would I have thought? First of all, *I would have known that somebody had made them; they had not just happened.* I would also have felt a sense of awe that somebody could do that; in fact, I do feel awe—and I was raised in a highly technical society. I am still amazed at all that can take place in those tiny watches.

What does this say to us? *It says to us that the God who is big enough for life is the God who is our Father. He is almighty. He is the One who is behind our existence, history, and future.* God is big enough to be trusted and worshiped and adored. Do we really believe in a God who is big enough for our life—and for eternity?

Chapter 2

THE FOCAL POINT OF FAITH

"I Believe . . . In Jesus Christ, His Only Son, Our Lord."

Anytime a person says, "I believe," he or she is implying that there is an objective truth in which he or she places confidence. If you say, "I believe in doctors," that means that you have confidence in medical practitioners and, when you are sick, you will consult one and follow his or her prescribed treatment. To say, "I believe in education" means that you have confidence that transmitting the knowledge of the past through instruction and practice is a beneficial thing to do. You believe that people gain from this process.

Periodically millions of Americans go to the polls to vote. They do this because they believe in the democratic process. The very act of voting is evidence of their faith. The person for whom they vote will be the person they *believe* will best promote what they perceive to be the program the city, county, or country should pursue.

Faith always has a focal point. The genuineness of a person's faith is expressed not only by verbal assent but by acting upon that faith. The sick person who does not consult a physician does not *really* believe in doctors. The person who does not send his children to school, or provide private tutoring for them, does not believe in education. The person who does not vote, when given the chance to do so, does not really believe in the democratic process.

An old story that I first heard as a boy impressed upon me what it meant to have faith. A great acrobat, who specialized in walking on tightropes, erected platforms on either side of Niagara Falls and stretched a well-anchored cable between the platforms. Thousands of people came to see him walk across Niagara Falls on the cable. With a long balance beam in his hand, the acrobat gingerly walked across on that narrow strand of wire. When he got back to the starting place, he got a wheelbarrow and pushed it across on the wire and back to his starting place. The crowd cheered his performance. Then he took two heavy sandbags, placed them in the wheelbarrow, and wheeled it across the cable and back.

The crowd was ecstatic with excitement. Then he turned to the crowd and asked, "Who believes that I can cross the wire with a person riding in the wheelbarrow?" As thousands of hands went up, he pointed to someone in the front row with her hand raised, and said, "Would you please get in?" The person who dared to get in the wheelbarrow was a true believer.

Now, the reality of our faith comes down to whether we are going to obey that to which we give intellectual assent. Do we really believe? If we do, then our actions will be based upon what we say we believe. The Christian faith as a religion and the Christian's faith as personal experience *come into focus in the person of Jesus Christ.* To profess faith in God is to believe in an abstract deity, and there are many non-Christian people around the world who believe in God. If you were to ask one of them to explain who his god is and what his god is like, you would find that this person believes in a different kind of god than the One in whom Christians believe. To say that we "believe in God the Father almighty, maker of heaven and earth," is to profess faith in a great philosophical first cause, or the ground of being. But that is not enough for the Christian. So when we say we believe in Jesus Christ, his only Son, our Lord," our faith is narrowing its focus down to that One who makes us Christian.

Paul wrote to the church in Colossae that Jesus Christ

is the image of the invisible God, the firstborn over all creation. For by Him were all things created; things in heaven and on earth, visible and invisible, whether thrones or powers or rulers or authorities; all things were created by Him and for Him. He is before all things, and in Him all things hold together. And He is the head of the body, the church; He is the beginning and the firstborn from among the dead, so that in everything He might have the supremacy. For God was pleased to have all His fullness dwell in Him and through Him to reconcile to Himself all things, whether things on earth or things in heaven, by making peace through His blood, shed on the cross" (Col. 1:15–20).

Jesus Christ is the focal point of the Christian's faith. The Christian faith is the person and work of Jesus Christ. And the person and work of Jesus Christ is the Christian faith.

When the Christian Indian mystic the Sadhu Sundar Singh was asked by his compatriots what he had found in Christianity that he could not find in the religions of his native land, his reply was "Jesus Christ." So, in this article of the Apostles' Creed we affirm that not only do we believe in God, whom we call Father, whom we describe with the adjective *Almighty,* who created the heavens and the earth, but we also understand that this infinite God has come down to a particular point in history and *shown himself to us* and identified with us. We understand that God has entered upon the stage of human history in the person of One we call Jesus, the Christ. *If we want to know what the invisible God is like, we must look at Jesus.*

What, then, are we affirming when we say we believe "in Jesus Christ, his only Son, our Lord"? Let us break that affirmation down into its four component phrases.

First, we say that we believe in *Jesus.* The name Jesus is the Greek form of the Hebrew name Yeshua, which means 'Jehovah saves!' The man who succeeded Moses as the leader of the Israelite people was named Joshua, 'Jehovah saves'. The Name 'Jesus' is the Greek form of that Hebrew name. This name tells us that God in Jesus Christ does what is necessary *to save* those who trust him.

Before Jesus was conceived, Mary was told by the angel that the power of the Holy Spirit would come upon her and that she would conceive and bear a child. When Joseph heard about her pregnancy he was prepared to divorce her. (According to Jewish law, an engagement could be broken only by divorce, because engagement in their culture was a more serious commitment than in ours.) But the angel appeared to Joseph in a dream and said to him, "Joseph, you are to marry Mary, and you are to name the baby, 'Jesus,' because *He will save His people from their sins*" (Matt. 1:18–25).

John the Baptist, seeing Jesus come to him, said; "Behold, the Lamb of God, Who takes away the sin of the world" (John 1:29). In the name of Jesus we understand that God has made provision for the salvation of lost humanity. Paul understood this when he wrote to the Colossian Christians, "For He has rescued us from the dominion of darkness and brought us into the kingdom of the Son He loves, in whom we have redemption, the forgiveness of sins" (Col. 1:13–14). The disciple John said the same thing: "For God so loved the world that He gave His one and only Son, that whoever believes in Him shall not perish but have eternal life" (John 3:16). The salvation that God offers the world is wrapped up in the person and work of this One in whom we affirm faith. That One is Jesus.

The second phrase in this affirmation is that Jesus is *the Christ*. The word *Christ* means "the anointed one' or "the messiah." In that title we have the fulfillment of all the Old Testament prophecies, which God gave through the prophets, that there would come One, his Anointed One, who would be a descendant of David and would be the King of Kings and Lord of Lords. The Jewish people tragically misunderstood this promise. They were looking for another king with political and military power, just like the first King David. They were not prepared for a king whose kingdom would not be a geographical, military, political, or economic kingdom. When Jesus said, "My kingdom is not of this world" (John 18:36), he was clearly saying that his kingdom had a different scope. But there were many people who wanted his kingdom to be of this world, and consequently they rejected him.

The kingdom that God set up in Jesus Christ is a kingdom ruled over by One whose subjects understand him to be King. They seek to follow him, and understand that his kingdom has no temporal limits. So they believe in Jesus Christ, the Savior who is the Anointed One, the Messiah, the fulfillment of all God's ancient promises to establish a kingdom, the citizens of which are the citizens of heaven.

The third facet of this affirmation in the Apostles' Creed is that we believe that Jesus, who is the Christ, also is *God's only Son*. We live in a world where we understand a son to be not only the logical but the sequential follower of a father. A male offspring resulting from the union of a wife and husband is called a son. In our way of thinking, a father in point of time precedes a son. That makes it hard for us to understand that our God is not limited by time.

Here we get into the mystery we call the Trinity. How can we believe that there is one God, and yet this God exists in three persons, the Father, the Son, and the Holy Spirit? Later we will discuss the Trinity. Here in this portion of the Apostles' Creed we are saying that we understand that if God is eternally the Father, then he eternally had to have a Son. If the Son is eternal, he had to be eternally related to the Father. The relationship of the Son to the Father is a relationship of honor, as the only Son is the One who is the inheritor of what the Father possesses. The Son also is of the same substance as the Father. When we say that we believe that Jesus Christ is God's only Son, we also are implying not only that he is of one substance with the Father, but—to use a more theological term—we are saying that we believe that Jesus is *divine*.

Now, what does that mean? There are two primary views in the stream of Christian thought. One of these goes back to Friedrich Schleiermacher in the nineteenth century, and was popularly voiced by Harry Emerson Fosdick of this century. That is, that in Christ humanity becomes God. Jesus Christ demonstrates for us how to utilize fully and to develop that divine spark with which all of us are born. He shows that by following his example and listening to his teachings, we too can experience that growth into the divine that Jesus pointed the way toward and in which he set the pace. In Christ, humanity becomes God.

Now, there is certainly an element of truth in this, because the Bible does tell us that Christ has set us an example on how to live. "Whoever claims to live in him must walk as Jesus did" wrote the apostle John (1 John 2:6). Jesus himself said "A new command I give you: Love one another. As I have loved you, so you must love one another" (John 13:34). He said that knowing that his love was going to lead him to the cross.

Yet the preponderance of Scripture indicates that this is only a partial view. Jesus Christ does set us an example. He does teach us about love: he shows us how to sacrifice and to give for the sake of others. But there is much more than that. If that is all that Jesus Christ did, he leaves us in hopeless despair, because who in the world can follow that example? The more orthodox, traditional view, which has its roots firmly founded in the New Testament, is that *in Christ, God became man.*

It makes all the difference in the world as to which of these we believe! Does Christ merely show us how a man can become God? That is the most despairing, bad news we could have. Who in the world can successfully follow that example?

The good news is the truth that in Christ, God became a man. The invisible God took upon himself flesh and blood and showed us what the invisible God is like. If we want to know what God is like, we are to look at the Son. If we want to know what it is to be loved by the Father, we are to accept the love of the Son. If we want to know what it is to be a part of the family of God, we are to accept the gracious gift of the Son's salvation. We do not have to earn it; we simply accept it. This, I suggest, is *really good news!* This puts the responsibility upon us, but it is not a responsibility of despair: it is a joyous opportunity of duty, the fulfilling duty by which we live.

But when we fall flat on our faces, he is still there to say, "I love you. Get up! Try again!" When the church confesses to belief in Jesus Christ, God's only-begotten Son, it confesses with Athanasius, "As the spring is not the stream, so the stream is not the spring. And yet both contain the same water which flows from the spring into the stream, even so the deity passes on from the Father to the Son without separation." In other words, we do not call the sun and its rays two lights. But the sun and its radiance are two. And yet the light is one; it proceeds from the sun and shines in all directions in its radiance. So it is that the deity of the Son is the same as that of the Father.

There is a mystery in this that we cannot begin fully to comprehend. The very heart of the Gospel contains this mystery: God eternally preexisted as Father, Son, and Holy Spirit. He chose to step into this world, and the One we know as the Son came into this world in human flesh. He took up residence here, but Bethlehem was not his beginning; it was merely the beginning of his independent existence as a man, as a human being.

As the Apostle Paul said, "Your attitude should be the same as that of Christ Jesus: Who, being in very nature God, did not consider equality with God something to be grasped, but made himself nothing, taking the very nature of a servant, being made in human likeness" (Phil. 2:5–7). What Paul indicates is that before Bethlehem, the Son had to make a decision, and his decision was to be obedient to the eternal counsels of the Father. He chose to come and be born; he lived as a servant and died for you and me. *In that marvelous fact is the good news that our God "reconciled us to himself through Jesus Christ"* (2 Cor. 5:18).

There is one final component of this affirmation in the Apostles' Creed. Having affirmed that we believe in Jesus, in Jesus the Christ, in Jesus Christ who is God's only Son, we then affirm that *he is our Lord!* It is interesting that in the Apostles' Creed the reference to Jesus as Savior is found only by implication, and that is in the name Jesus. The affirmation we make in this confession of faith is that Jesus is Lord. There is a trap in evangelism into which it is easy to fall. This is the trap of thinking that the mere recitation of a formula indicating belief in Jesus Christ as Savior and Lord is adequate for eternal salvation. But the recitation in itself is inadequate. Remember that the emphasis placed by the Apostles' Creed is not on Jesus as Savior, but rather on Jesus as *Lord*. After all, no one wants to go to hell. If by repeating some formula we can affirm that Jesus is our Savior and think that thereby we have somehow secured eternal fire insurance, we have latched onto Jesus Christ just so that he will do something for us. But when we sincerely say that we believe that Jesus is our Lord, we are bowing prostrate at the feet of the One who is the King of Kings and Lord of Lords! He is our ruler; he is our Sovereign; he is the One who has absolute control of our lives. We thank him for taking control of our lives, for we know that his plans and purposes for our lives are better than anything of which we could dream. In declaring him our Lord we acknowledge that we are merely the stewards of what he puts into our hands—our time, our talents, our gifts, our influence—for everything we have belongs to Him. If Jesus Christ is our Lord, we do not have to worry about him being our Savior. But if he is not our Lord, he cannot truly be our Savior.

What does Jesus save us from? We will discuss that question in more detail in a later chapter, but for now let's touch on three aspects of the salvation Jesus brings us.

First, Jesus saves us from the despair of godlessness.

In George MacDonald's novel *The Tutor's First Love,* Hugh Sutherland falls in love with lovely Euphra, who is under the influence of an evil man. "Hugh," asks Euphra, "do you think there is a God?"

Hugh is not certain, but he remembers a good man who believes in God and offers to put Euphra in touch with this man. "I will write down his address for you. But what can he save you from?"

"From no God," she answers. "If there is no God, then I am sure there is a devil and that he has got me in his power."[1]

No one can doubt the reality of evil in this world. Our world, our cities, and our hearts are full of it. The first thing from which Jesus saves us is the futility that comes from there not being a God to counter the evil.

Second, Jesus saves us from sin. The result of sin—eternal death—is reversed by the life, death, and resurrection of Jesus Christ. By his life Jesus showed us what right living is. By his death Jesus took upon himself the penalty for our sins. By his resurrection he guarantees victory for us over the worst that sin can do to those who trust him, which is physical death.

And third, Jesus saves us from hopelessness. Because of Jesus believers can be assured of a future. Good works pay off because God doesn't let goodness go unnoticed. Bravery pays off because the ultimate cost of bravery, which is death, is but an investment in life in eternity. Truth pays off because God is on the side of truth. Faithfulness pays off because the result is a crown of life (Rev. 2:10).

Jesus says, "Not every one that says to me, 'Lord, Lord,' shall enter the kingdom of heaven, but he who does the will of My Father, Who is in heaven" (Matt. 7:21). What does it mean to do the will of the Father who is in heaven except to accept his revealed will and act upon it, and what is that but obedience? And what is obedience but to put the running of our lives into the hands of our risen Lord?

"I believe . . . in Jesus Christ, his only Son, our Lord." Think about the implications of those words for our lives. If Jesus Christ is Lord as the New Testament teaches he is, he is sovereign. Thus the focal point of our faith is this One who invaded this world so many years ago, who lived, who taught, who performed miracles, who died on a cross and on the third day rose again, who now has ascended to the right hand of God the Father almighty, and who, if he is our Lord, we can trust to be our Savior!

NOTES

1. George MacDonald, *The Tutor's First Love* (Minneapolis: Bethany House Publishers, 1984), 161. (Originally published under the title *David Elginbrod* [London: Hurst & Blackett, 1863].)

Chapter 3

HOW DID GOD BECOME MAN?

"I believe . . . In Jesus Christ, . . . Who Was Conceived by the Holy Ghost, Born of the Virgin Mary."

Does it really make any difference how Jesus Christ was born? Couldn't God just have overwhelmed someone with God and made any human being God?

This sounds plausible, for after all, God being God almighty, could do anything. Right?

Wrong!

God can function only in a way that is true to his nature; otherwise he destroys his integrity. For God to do something out of keeping with his nature would be an intolerable contradiction of his character. God is love; for him to do something unloving would destroy the integrity of his love. God is also truth; if he were to lie, his veracity would be destroyed.

Therefore for God to become a man, he had to do so in a way that did not take away from his true deity nor override the freedom of human nature. If his death was to cover all the sins of humanity, he had to have dimensions approaching infinity. If he died for us as sinners, then he had to be fully human in order to identify fully with us as sinners.

So the question of the virgin birth of Jesus Christ concerns much more than just biology. It has profound theological implications. How can we know what God is like? What was God accomplishing by becoming a man?

The Apostles' Creed says simply that Jesus "was conceived by the Holy Ghost, born of the Virgin Mary." Taken at its face value this means that Jesus was conceived in the womb of Mary, who was a virgin, and that conception was accomplished by the Holy Spirit without the aid of a human father.

Now, the doctrine of the virgin birth does not refer to the biological process called parthenogenesis, which *The Random House Dictionary* defines as "development of an egg without fertilization."[1] Rather, this doctrine refers to the conception and birth of Jesus from a human mother and a divine Father. The doctrine of the virgin birth also does not refer to the Roman Catholic doctrine of the immaculate conception. This idea was proclaimed by the pope in 1854, affirming that Mary, the mother of Jesus, was herself conceived without any taint of sin. By this affirmation the Roman Catholic church tried to solve the dilemma of original sin in Jesus. If he had a human, and therefore sinful, mother, then Jesus must have inherited her sinful nature. But if she were conceived without sin, then she had no sinful nature to pass on to her Son. The Catholic church proclaimed that from the first instant of her conception in the womb of her mother, Saint Anne, Mary was free from all stain of original sin. The Roman Catholic church felt this solved the problem of the hereditary effects of sin in the nature of Jesus.

Stripped of the accumulated elaborations by theologians, what is the biblical evidence for the doctrine of the virgin birth? The virgin birth is mentioned only twice in the New Testament, by Matthew and Luke, whereas the writers of the Gospels of Mark and John, and the Apostle Paul in his letters, make no mention of it. In Matthew 1:18 we read

This is how the birth of Jesus Christ came about. His mother, Mary, was pledged to be married to Joseph, but before they came together, she was found to be with child through the Holy Spirit.

The second reference is in Luke 1:26–38, where we read

In the sixth month, God sent the angel Gabriel to Nazareth, a town in Galilee, to a virgin pledged to be married to a man named Joseph, a descendant of David. The virgin's name was Mary. The angel went to her and said, "Greetings, you who are highly favored! The Lord is with you." Mary was greatly troubled at his words and wondered what kind of greeting this might be. But the angel said to her, "Do not be afraid, Mary, you have found favor with God. You will be with child and give birth to a son, and you are to give him the name Jesus. He will be great and will be called the Son of the Most High. The Lord God will give him the throne of his father David, and he will reign over the house of Jacob forever; his kingdom will never end."

"How will this be," Mary asked the angel, "since I am a virgin?"

The angel answered, "The Holy Spirit will come upon you, and the power of the Most High will overshadow you. So the holy one to be born will be called the Son of God. Even Elizabeth your relative is going to have a child in her old age, and she who was said to be barren is in her sixth month. For nothing is impossible with God."

"I am the Lord's servant," Mary answered. "May it be to me as you have said." Then the angel left her.

But to put the question of the virgin birth of Jesus in proper perspective, another question must be answered: Was the conception and birth of Jesus the beginning of Jesus Christ?

The New Testament's answer to that question is clearly no! John, in his Gospel, stated, "In the beginning was the Word, and the Word was with God, and the Word was God. He was with God in the beginning" (John 1:1-2). "The Word became flesh and made his dwelling among us. We have seen his glory, the glory of the One and Only, who came from the Father, full of grace and truth" (John 1:14). The Son of God, existing as the expression of the Father, the Word, was alive before he was born into this world. He "became flesh and dwelt among us." Also, in John 5:8, Jesus said to the Pharisees, "Before Abraham was, I am." He stated to them something that they understood; namely, that the Jehovah God of the Old Testament, who had revealed himself to Moses as the great I Am, was the God with whom Jesus identified himself. For that reason they sought to stone him, because they believed him to be guilty of blasphemy.

Paul, in Galatians 4:4, says, "When the time had fully come, God sent His Son born of a woman." The very clear meaning of the

Greek word translated as "sent" is "to go from one place to another." God indeed sent his Son born of a woman. Then, in Philippians 2:5–7, Paul, appealing to the Christians to adopt an attitude of self-sacrificing service, writes, "Your attitude should be the same as that of Jesus Christ, who, being in very nature God, did not consider equality with God something to be grasped (clung to) but made Himself nothing, taking the very nature of a servant, being made in human likeness."

Thus the full question that must be answered is not just how was the Person whom we know in history as Jesus Christ born, but also *how did God become a human being?* The affirmation that Jesus Christ was conceived by the Holy Spirit and born of the Virgin Mary is the creed's answer to that question.

Why is it difficult for some people to believe that Jesus was born of a virgin?

There are three main reasons: some people object to the doctrine of the virgin birth because of its supernatural element; others object because of the silence of Mark and John and Paul; and still others object because Greek mythology also speaks of supernatural births for people of prominence. Let us examine these objections to see if we may clear away some of these stumbling blocks which hinder our faith.

First, if the virgin birth is true, it is obviously a supernatural event. Some people object to the supernatural because they say that God just does not work that way. But those who object to the doctrine of the virgin birth because it is supernatural must also deny or find naturalistic explanations for many other events in the biblical narrative. Creation was a supernatural event, as was the flood, the exodus and all of the events that surrounded it, and the prophesying in the Old Testament. In the New Testament the supernatural abounds: Jesus fed the five thousand, healed the lepers, raised Lazarus from the dead, walked on the sea, and himself rose from the dead. All of these events were supernatural. These would all have to be denied if the virgin birth was denied because it was a supernatural event. Thus if this objection is true and if we must not believe that the virgin birth is real because it is a supernatural event and God does not work that way, then Christianity is a hoax, a fraud, a lie; and prayer is nothing more than a pious exercise whose only value lies in its psychological effect! This objection, then, is invalid.

There are others who claim that the virgin birth really should be questioned because Mark and John and Paul say nothing about it. Their silence is a fact. Matthew and Luke are the only two New Testament writers who mention the virgin birth of Jesus Christ. Yet, Mark's Gospel was probably the first gospel written and is silent on the subject. John does not mention it, and neither does Paul.

Why?

The purpose of Mark's Gospel is to narrate the events of Jesus' ministry; his story, therefore, begins with the baptism of Jesus by John the Baptizer. Mark makes no mention of anything prior to the baptism of Jesus. And John does not tell of the earthly origins of Jesus, saying, "In the beginning was the Word, and the Word was with God, and the Word was God, and the Word became flesh." That is the keynote of John's gospel. And John, who provides us in his Gospel with much material that is omitted from the other three gospels, *says nothing to contradict* the narrative of the birth of Jesus found in Matthew and Luke.

"Evidently Paul knew nothing of it," say the critics, "or else he surely would have mentioned it." But would he? Paul did not make mention of any of the facts of Jesus' life on earth. Matthew, Mark, Luke, and John had already done that; Paul taught the significance of Christ's death and resurrection for our salvation. So this second argument against the virgin birth has no substance.

The third objection to the validity of Jesus' virgin birth is the belief that almost all great religious leaders—Moses, Confucius, and Mohammed being exceptions—were claimed by ancient nations to have been born in some supernatural manner. Thus it is inferred that the disciples, looking back on the greatness of Jesus Christ, concluded that only a supernatural beginning could fit this man.

Two responses can counter this objection. First, great Greek poets, such as Aeschylus and Sophocles, and the best of the Roman authors, such as Cicero, repudiated those myths as too sensuous and immoral to have any religious credibility. Now, if Greeks and Romans of renown said such myths were beneath the ethical standards of their gods, is it really plausible to believe that the early Christians would have used a fabrication of a supernatural beginning to bolster faith in Jesus Christ in the eyes of the Greeks and the Romans, to whom that early church went with the Good News? Second, Luke and Acts were both written by Luke, a medical doctor. We know that Acts was written before 64 A.D., and the Gospel of Luke was written prior to that time because the book of Acts is a subsequent letter to Theophilus, following up on what Luke had already written in the Gospel. That means that Mary was very probably still living when Luke wrote his Gospel and the book of Acts. Also, many other disciples were still living who knew Jesus quite well and could have refuted any such base claim as the virgin birth, had it not been a fact.

Additional reasons for belief in the virgin birth are several. In Acts 1:1-4 Luke states that he went to the very sources in order to check out the truth of what he writes. That was done at an early date in the young church's history. Paul states in Romans 1:4 that the resurrection proved the deity of Jesus Christ. Luke states in Acts 2 that Pentecost came and convinced all of the disciples of the importance of Jesus' resurrection, and he also states that Mary was filled with the Holy Spirit at Pentecost. And because Mary was filled with the Holy Spirit at Pentecost she came to an understanding of the full import of what the angel had said to her, that the Holy One begotten in her would be called the Son of God.

Let us remember that the penalty for moral promiscuity in that day was death by stoning. Mary certainly would not have gone around broadcasting the fact, "Guess what! I'm pregnant, and the Holy Spirit did it." We know she would not have done that, for that is psychologically and historically out of place for her. It was not until Pentecost that she fully understood what had happened.

When the infant church became convinced of the deity of Jesus, it began to inquire into his human origin. Luke, the careful historian, says that Mary did not at first understand the angel's pronouncement to her, and that she went to talk it over with her cousin

Elizabeth. Matthew adds that Joseph did not grasp the facts when he was first acquainted with this startling news. After Pentecost, however, Mary no longer needed to hide all the information that she had kept as a secret deep in her heart. The deity of Jesus Christ, which was proved by the resurrection, necessitated a full understanding of who he was, and his supernatural birth then underscored the reality of his deity. John and Paul emphasize that Jesus Christ was in the beginning with God and that he became human. Matthew and Luke tell us how he became human.

Now, by way of comparison I can say that being a man, I became a husband; or, being a man, I became a father; or, being a man, I became a minister. Nothing is changed or lost in my essential nature, but something is added by way of function. Thus when the Scripture says, "In the beginning was the Word, and the Word was with God, and the Word was God, and *the Word became flesh," this does not indicate any change in the essential nature of Jesus, the Christ.* And understand that this One who was "in very nature God, not think likeness with God was to be hung on to . . . emptied Himself and came in the likeness of man."

Now what does this mean for us today? Is there any practical consequence for us living in this twentieth century other than just theological argumentation? Does the doctrine of the virgin birth have any practical consequences for us?

Let me point out three.

First, it is important and significant for us to understand that because Jesus was the heavenly child of an earthly mother and the earthly child of a heavenly Father, the combination of the human and divine natures in the one Person, Jesus Christ, makes him the perfect revealer of God in terms that human beings can understand. Paul wrote that God "made his light shine in our hearts to give us the light of the knowledge of the glory of God in the face of Jesus Christ" (2 Cor. 4:6).

Second, because Jesus was the heavenly child of an earthly mother and the earthly child of a heavenly Father, this combination of the human and the divine natures of Jesus makes him the perfect mediator between us and God. He was truly human because of his mother. Yet he was also truly divine because of his heavenly Father. Because he lived a life without sin, this qualified him uniquely to be the perfect Savior and Redeemer. If Jesus had been only a man, his goodness would have saved no one but himself. If Jesus had been only divine masquerading as a human being, then his goodness would have been an unattainable example, in no way applicable to us mortals. But because Jesus was truly human and truly divine, he thus was uniquely suited to be our mediator. Only he can stand as an intermediary between us and God, "able to be touched with the feelings of our infirmities, in every way tempted just as you and I are tempted, and yet without sin" (Heb. 4:15–16).

When we look at the universe that God has created, it is easy to think of our own insignificance and unimportance. If all we see is the universe observed through the eye of a telescope or through the lens of a microscope, we might conclude that we are unimportant in God's scheme of things. But when we understand that God thought enough of you and of me and of the whole world to come and take up residence here, we can then be impressed with the fact that *God is not remote*. God is *personal*. He is *immanent*. He is *here*. We also understand that when we want to come to God, we have a mediator who shares in our human nature. He understands our weaknesses; he understands our needs. He is perfectly able to represent us before our heavenly Father. That, indeed, is powerful and meaningful to us today!

The third practical application of this doctrine of the virgin birth is that the reality of the virgin birth stands as the first sign and the initial illustration of the supernatural power that is the Good News, the gospel of supernatural love, the gospel of supernatural redemption, the gospel of supernatural hope! If God can inject himself into human history by means of a young Jewish woman so that his son is born not of natural descent, nor of human decision, nor of a husband's will, but is born of God, then we can be encouraged to believe that this same God can inject himself into our dead, sinful human nature and produce new lives that also make us children of God! That is what we need. That is what John said Jesus came to do: "to all who received him, to those who believed in his name, he gave the right to become children of God—children born not of natural descent, nor of human decision or a husband's will, but born of

God" (John 1:12–13). What Jesus said to Nicodemus takes on new significance, for, if we all must be "born again" (the Greek word means "anew" or "from above") to enter the kingdom of God, then we can find hope and strength in knowing that because Jesus was born supernaturally into the human family, we can be born supernaturally into the family of God!

I believe in the virgin birth, not because I understand how it happened, but because I trust the witness of Matthew and Luke. I believe in the virgin birth because I find this consistent with believing in "God the Father almighty, Maker of heaven and earth." I find it easy to believe that the early church was so morally pure and so righteous in its teaching that it would not have perpetrated upon the world such a doctrine if it had not been true. I also believe in the virgin birth because I find it extremely difficult to believe the contrary—that Mary was a morally loose woman and that Jesus was a bastard. I cannot believe that. In light of the life and ministry and teaching of Jesus Christ, and in what we know of the gospel record, I find it much easier to believe that Jesus was indeed "conceived by the Holy Ghost, born of the Virgin Mary."

Do you find that too hard to believe? I hope not.

In conclusion, I want to make it plain that you do not *have* to believe in the virgin birth to be a Christian. Such rejection, however, leaves faith incomplete and less than biblical. What makes a person a Christian is that person's faith, trust, confidence in Jesus Christ as his or her own Lord and Savior. But on what evidence do we put our faith and trust in Jesus Christ as our Lord and Savior? Is it not the evidence found in the New Testament? Then how can we reject the evidence from that same New Testament concerning the virgin birth of Jesus? The book that tells us how we can become children of God also tells us how the Son of God became a man.

Because God could do that, he can also produce new life in all of those who will trust him.

NOTES

1. *The Random House Dictionary of the English Language*, 2d ed., S.V. "parthenogenesis."

Chapter 4

WHY A CRIMINAL'S DEATH?

"I Believe . . . In Jesus Christ, . . . Who Suffered Under Pontius Pilate, Was Crucified, Dead, and Buried."

Which do you think is more important? The life and teachings of Jesus, or the death and resurrection of Jesus? Maybe you feel that this is an unnecessary division of the total impact of Jesus on this world. Let me ask the question a little differently. When you think of Jesus Christ, do you think primarily of his life and teachings, or do you think primarily of his death and resurrection?

Some Christians concentrate all their attention on the life and teachings of Jesus. Such people often view his death as an unfortunate end for a courageous rebel who dared to challenge the religious establishment, which was committed to the status quo. On the other hand, some Christians virtually ignore the teachings of Jesus and concentrate all of their attention on the death and resurrection of our Lord. They emphasize the eternal benefits that are made available to us and pay almost no attention to the moral and ethical dimensions of what Jesus taught.

The Apostles' Creed leaves no doubt where the early church placed its emphasis. The creed, after affirming that Jesus Christ, God's only-begotten Son, "was conceived by the Holy Ghost, born of the Virgin Mary," omits any reference to his life and teachings. It skips over to, "suffered under Pontius Pilate, was crucified, dead, and buried."

Does this mean that the early Christians thought that the life and teachings of Jesus were unimportant? Not at all! But the manner in

which the Apostles' Creed is worded does give us insight into how
the early Christians understood Jesus' mission and impact on this
world, and the implications for those who seek to follow him.

Does this mean that modern Christians should ignore the life and
teachings of Jesus?

Before going further, I'd like to point out that if it were not for the
affirmation of the Apostles' Creed that concerns the resurrection,
references to Jesus' life and death would mean little to us. And, in
fact, there would be no Christian church. When considering the
death of Jesus versus the life and teachings of Jesus, remember that
all of these must be measured in the light of his resurrection.

Why does the creed skip all references to the life and teachings of
Jesus? Did the early church consider that somehow they really were
not important? What should be our approach to understanding the
life and teachings of our Lord? The silence of the Apostles' Creed on
the life and teachings of Jesus does not indicate that the Apostles
thought that his life and teachings were of no importance. What
the creed does is give us perspective on the total ministry of Jesus.
The teachings of Jesus were not his mission to the world. The
primary mission of Jesus was the cross. His teachings and his
miracles were what happened on the way to Calvary. Jesus came
to die!

Lest you think that is too narrow an interpretation of the primary
thrust of Jesus' life, let me remind you that John the Baptizer announced to the assembled crowd at Jesus' baptism, "Behold, the
Lamb of God, Who takes away the sin of the world" (John 1:29).
There was no question in the minds of those who heard John that
when John referred to the Lamb of God, who takes away the sin of
the world, he was talking about death. Jesus said about himself that
he had not come to be served, but to serve and to give his life as
ransom for many (Matt. 20:28 and Mark 10:45). When the Apostles
preached the gospel at Pentecost, and when they traveled, proclaim-
ing the Good News, their message centered on the death and resurrection of Jesus. The Good News they preached was that sin's guilt
had been atoned for on the cross. The fear of death had been re-

moved by the resurrection. The hope of eternal life had become a reality, because Jesus had died on a cross as a common criminal, and God had raised him from the dead. Furthermore, the Apostle Paul, in writing to one of the churches he had visited, explained his ministry to the church members by saying, "I determine to know nothing among you except Jesus Christ and Him crucified" (1 Cor. 2:2).

Not a word about the Sermon on the Mount. Not a word about the healing of the sick. Not a word about the raising of Lazarus from the dead. Not a word about the feeding of the five thousand. What are we to make of that silence?

To understand the perspective from which the early Apostles viewed the life and work of Jesus, imagine yourself in their shoes. Each of them had been engaged in some kind of secular profession. Some were tax collectors, others were fishers. Whatever their secular profession, there wasn't a religious professional among them. Jesus had come across each man's path and each man had discerned in Jesus something unusual. Each man had responded to Jesus' call when he said, "Follow Me, and I will make you become fishers of men" (Matt. 4:19 and Mark 1:17). The men left their businesses, their families, their communities; and for three years they followed him across the hills, valleys, and plains of Palestine. They heard him teach; they heard the Sermon on the Mount; they heard what he had to say in opposition to the Pharisees. They watched him heal the sick and straighten the legs of a lame man. They watched him as he restored sight to the blind, as he raised the dead, and as he multiplied the bread and the fishes for the multitudes. They saw him walk on the water. They knew that there was something extraordinary about this Man. But their hopes in Jesus had to do with their earthly political, economic, and social ambitions.

Here was a man who could solve the problems of society. He would make a grand king. The problems of hunger, disease, and natural catastrophe were all in his power to banish. Even dead people could be brought back to life. With that kind of power and the popularity such power would command, the hated Romans could be driven out of the country; and the nation could be once again the free and powerful monarchy that it had been in the glorious days of David.

Then the Apostles walked with him to Jerusalem, saw him betrayed, listened from afar as he was tried; and they watched from a distance as he was nailed to a cross. When the cross was raised and dropped with a thud into that hole on top of Golgotha's hill, they saw the violent jolt that drained his life from his body and tore their dream from their hearts. Slowly he died. There was no question that he was dead, and when his body was taken from that cross, loving hands took him and wrapped him in burial clothes and took him to a tomb that a wealthy follower had allowed them to use.

These men mourned more than the death of a friend. They mourned the passing of a dream, the dashing of hopes of glory. They were disillusioned and frustrated. They were also frightened. It was clear that they were vulnerable to the same political and religious powers who had killed their leader.

The next day was the Sabbath. According to Jewish law, nothing could be done for the body on that day. But on the third day, Sunday, some women went to the tomb, a cave in the side of a hill, to provide the ointment and the spices that were traditionally used in the wrapping of the body. When they stooped to go into the cave, his body was not there. An angel said, "Why are you looking for the living among the dead; He is not here, He is risen as He told you. He has gone before you" (Luke 24:5–6).

Then Jesus began appearing to the disciples. He joined two as they walked to Emmaus and then appeared to the eleven gathered in an upper room, and then appeared to more than five hundred assembled in one place. They saw him, heard him speak, and even touched him. For a period of more than forty days he taught them and they listened to him. But it was not until Pentecost that they fully understood. The most significant thing that happened in their minds, in their faith, and in their focus was that they came to an understanding that this Jesus was indeed the Son of God. He had indeed "given His life as a ransom for many," freeing those who believed from captivity to the evil one. The resurrection had broken the bonds of fear of death.

It was in the light of the death and resurrection of Jesus after Pentecost that the disciples could go back and review the significance of his life and his teachings. Their examination of what he said and what he did in his earthly ministry was informed by the cross and the empty tomb.

And when they went out from Jerusalem around the world, what was their message? They did not talk about the miracle worker, they did not talk about this One who could heal, who could feed the hungry, who could restore sight to the blind. They talked about Jesus who was crucified, dead and buried, and rose again.

The disciples reviewed Jesus' life and then recorded the significant events of his life for us to read in the Gospel narratives. We find in the Gospel that Jesus was at times quite reticent about the miracles he performed. He cured a man of leprosy and he said, "Do not tell anybody what happened" (Matt. 8:2–4). Why? Because Jesus knew that this would focus the attention of the people on the wrong thing. He had not come primarily to heal or to feed, though he had the power to do both. He had come to die!

Shortly after his baptism by John, Jesus was led by the Holy Spirit into the wilderness, where he was tempted by Satan. The devil wanted to divert Jesus from his primary task. The devil offered Jesus all of the attention, all of the acclamation, all of the following, he could want. He could have the world and avoid the cross just by worhiping Satan. The devil tried to get Jesus to use his miraculous powers for selfish ends, and tried to sidetrack his use of faith in order to keep Jesus from the cross.

No wonder, then, that when the disciples went out to preach, they preached the death and the resurrection of Jesus Christ. Why is the suffering and death of Jesus the starting point for understanding the work of Jesus? That is the starting point because God is holy. Sin is horrendous! Sinners are hopeless! God created human beings in his likeness that we might love him and fellowship with him. But sin became the great separator. It still is. Sin is still that thing which separates a person from God, separates a person from other people, and separates a person from his or her best self. Sin horribly marred the beauty of God's creative work. Because God is absolutely holy and righteous, sinners cannot enter his presence. It is only when that sin has been atoned for, forgiven, and blotted out that you and I can stand before the presence of a holy God.

So Jesus Christ came to die, to deal with the most fundamental problem that any of us has—the problem of our sin and our consequent guilt before the presence of a holy and righteous God. It was our sin that led Jesus Christ to the cross.

When Jesus "suffered under Pontius Pilate," how did he suffer? Jesus Christ endured in that last week, particularly in the last two days, all of the suffering to which you and I can be subjected. He suffered, first of all, being misunderstood by the religious leaders. He suffered being misunderstood by the community at large. He suffered being forsaken by his family and friends. He suffered the most gross form of injustice at the hands of Caiaphas, the high priest, and also Pontius Pilate, the civil judge. He suffered physically. He suffered psychologically. And in the final moment, the outcry on the cross when he said, "My God, My God, why have You forsaken Me?" he revealed how he suffered the ultimate in spiritual pain.

When the writers of the creed say, "suffered under Pontius Pilate," they pinpoint his suffering at a specific time in history. Jesus suffered on earth under the rule of a Roman ruler named Pontius Pilate. Christianity is based on historic fact. It is not based on a myth. It is not somebody's fairy tale. It started at a particular place in a particular time. Furthermore, when the creed calls attention to the fact that he suffered under Pontius Pilate, it calls attention to the judicial character of Christ's death.

There are three views of sin: the educational view, the medical view, and the judicial view. The educational view looks upon sin as immaturity. It has to be outgrown. Sin is simply that which a person does because he or she has not learned enough, not grown enough, not matured enough. Then there is the medical view of sin. Sin is a disease. It is something that has to be cured, generally through psychotherapy. To be sure, sin is immaturity, and sin causes much "dis-ease." But these two views of sin, although true in part, miss the real point of the death of Jesus.

Sin is any failure to live up to God's expectations; it is a breaking of his law. It was appropriate for sin, as the breaking of the law, to be dealt with (even though unfairly) in a court of law with a judge, Pontius Pilate, presiding. Sin is transgression. Because the law is broken, the law must be satisfied. So Jesus was tried and sentenced by two courts, the religious court, presided over by Caiaphas, and the civil court, presided over by Pontius Pilate. The civil court, with its power to free or condemn, condemned Jesus to death. When a criminal is sentenced by a court, the penalty is the payment exacted for the crime. He or she has broken the law and has to pay the penalty. If the law is a capital crime, then he or she has to pay a capital sentence. Had Jesus died of a heart attack, that would have been merely an untimely demise of a promising man. Had he been killed in an accident, that would have been an unfortunate occurrence. But in fact he was sentenced to die as a criminal by a court of law. And because he had no sin of his own, he could take our sins upon himself.

Let me relate a parable. A young man lived in a large community. He was raised in a family that loved him, but he showed early signs of rebelliousness. When he reached his teenage years he wanted nothing more to do with his mother and father, his sisters and brothers; so he left home. The family tried to keep in touch with him, but he resisted all attempts; so they finally gave up. But the parents occasionally would hear word drifting back about his misbehavior. He drank too much, partied too much, drove too fast, and was generally engaged in the kind of antisocial behavior that leads to serious trouble. This was all the more painful because his father was a judge, and the boy was flaunting in his father's face everything that the father thought important about civilized living.

One day the boy was involved in an accident that caused considerable damage. It was a repeat offense, and there was no question as to who was at fault. The boy was arrested, put in jail overnight, and the next day was brought before the court. As the boy walked in, whom should he find sitting behind the bench but his father, whom he had not seen for several years. The son hung his head in embarrassment, but inwardly there flickered a spark of hope that he might get off with a light sentence.

Although dissipation and careless living had changed the boy's appearance, his father recognized him. But knowing that he had to do the work of a judge, he sat impassively behind the bench and passed sentence on the boy. He assessed the stiffest fine, told the boy that he must pay all of the damages, and sentenced him to thirty days in jail. The boy was crushed, for he had no resources with which to pay the fine or the damages, and he was fearful of going to jail.

After passing sentence the father arose from his judge's chair and went around in front of the bench to where his son was standing. He took off his robes, reached into his pocket, pulled out his checkbook, and wrote a check to cover the fine and the damages. Then he said, "Son, you have broken the law and I have exacted the penalty that the law requires, but I love you and I always have and I want you to know it. That is why I am paying your penalty." And with that the father went to jail to serve the thirty days.

That is an imperfect picture of what God has done for us. A holy and righteous God, he must exact the penalty for sin, which has offended his holy standards. But in his love he has stepped out from behind the bench of divine judgment, and, in the person of his Son, Jesus Christ, he has paid the penalty for your sins and mine.

Why does the creed say "buried"? Because burial is the final seal of death. Jesus had a real body, and real dead bodies are buried. The burial of the body was the prelude to the resurrection of the body, and this is the way the creed reminds us that this One, who suffered under Pontius Pilate at a particular point in history, was a real person. He has dealt with our real problems, our real sins. He was buried with a real body and he was raised with a real body. Those of us who put our trust in him need never again be afraid of death, for Jesus "suffered under Pontius Pilate, was crucified, dead, and buried."

Chapter 5

WHERE WAS JESUS WHILE HIS BODY WAS IN THE GRAVE?

"He Descended Into Hell."

Where was Jesus while his body was in the grave?

What does the phrase "He descended into hell" mean? Why do some churches include the phrase and others omit it?

Before we discuss these questions, it is important to stress that although there are many things God has revealed to us in the Holy Scriptures, there is much that God has not seen fit to reveal to us. The writers of the Bible were inspired to reveal everything that we need to know and believe in order to be brought into a right relationship with God.

The Westminster Shorter Catechism asks, "What do the Scriptures principally teach?" It answers, "The Scriptures principally teach what man is to believe concerning God, and what duty God requires of man." Not all of the mysteries of the universe are made clear in the Bible. Not all of the closets of potential knowledge are unlocked by the Bible. It is, in the words of William Walsham How, in his hymn "O Word of God Incarnate," written in 1867,

> the chart and compass that o'er life's surging sea
> 'mid mists and rocks and quicksands
> still guides, O Christ, to Thee.

Tourists are always taken on tours of the local housing extravaganza. In Vienna, it is the Schönbrunn Palace. In Versailles, it is the Versailles Palace. In Beijing, China, it is the Forbidden City. In the middle of nowhere in South Germany, it is the Neuschwanstein

Castle. It is hard to imagine that a family ever lived in one of those magnificent places. These homes are huge, extravagantly huge, designed more for housing egos than people. There are exquisite brocades and tapestries, murals on the walls, gold and marble in abundance, rooms for entertaining hundreds, and ingenious devices for heating, supplying water, and providing other amenities.

Several years ago, while going through the Schönbrunn Palace in Vienna, a tragicomic picture flashed through my mind. A little boy was standing in one of those vast halls crying, "Daddy," not knowing where in the vast arrangement of rooms to start looking. It might take a three-day safari just to get a bedtime story. In my mind's eye I could see that little chap frantically running through the cavernous rooms and down the endless hallways, opening a multitude of doors, and at those doors that would not open, looking through the keyholes to see if Daddy was in there.

Then I thought, That is something of a parable of life. We are children who are lost, looking for Daddy, searching through the rooms of the universe, opening doors to knowledge, peering through keyholes into rooms that are locked. Yet our Father has given us a book that contains the instructions on how to find him. The Bible is not a guidebook to the universe; it is a guide to God. There are closets in life that remain locked, even whole rooms that cannot be opened. Some of them have keyholes through which we may peek; and when we do so, we get only a hint of what lies beyond the doors.

It is important for us to limit ourselves to what God has revealed and not set forth dogma on those things that God has not made plain. We should draw limited conclusions from limited evidence.

This is a roundabout way of leading up to the answer to the question, Where was Jesus while his body was in the grave? The frank answer to that question is, We are not sure. Jesus said to the thief on the adjacent cross, "Today you will be with me in paradise" (Luke 23:43). But because the biblical word *day* does not always mean a twenty-four-hour period, we are still uncertain about where Jesus' soul went while his body was in the grave.

But the Apostle Peter, in his first epistle, gives us a keyhole glimpse of what took place, and the Creed's phrase "He descended into hell" is an early church affirmation of what Jesus Christ did for us by his death.

Peter writes,

For Christ died for sins once for all, the righteous for the unrighteous, to bring you to God. He was put to death in the body but made alive by the Spirit, through whom also he went and preached to the spirits in prison who disobeyed long ago when God waited patiently in the days of Noah while the ark was being built. In it only a few people, eight in all, were saved through water, and this water symbolized baptism that now saves you also—not the removal of dirt from the body but the pledge of a good conscience toward God. It saves you by the resurrection of Jesus Christ, who has gone into heaven and is at God's right hand—with angels, authorities and powers in submission to him. (1 Pet. 3:18–22)

This phrase, "He descended into hell," was not in the Apostles' Creed as early or as universally as the other phrases that are found there. It was first used in the Aquillian form of the creed about A.D. 390 and appeared as "descended into inferna." Some Greek translations used the word *hades* for *inferna,* and others used the phrase, *lower parts.* Some forms of the creed in which these words were found did not mention the burial of Christ, but the Roman and Middle Eastern forms generally mentioned the burial but not the descent into hades. This seems to indicate that many of the early Christians understood the two phrases to mean the same thing, in which case after saying, "He was crucified, dead, and buried" to say, "He descended into hell" would have been redundant, for it referred to entering into the lower parts, or the grave.

Later on, however, the Roman form of the creed added, "He descended into hell" after it mentioned the burial. John Calvin argued that for those who added the phrase, it must have denoted something additional. Remember, however, that the phrase is not found anywhere in the Bible, and those words are not based on such clear, direct statements of the Bible as are the other articles of the creed. So where did the idea originate?

There are four passages in Scripture on which the idea of the descent into hell may be based. Two of them are in 1 Peter. But let us look first at the two that are not in Peter's letter.

The first passage is in Psalm 16:9–10, which is quoted by Peter in his sermon on the day of Pentecost as applicable to Jesus. It reads, "Therefore my heart is glad, and my tongue rejoices. My body also will rest secure, because You will not abandon me to Sheol, nor will You let Your Holy One see decay." What does the word *Sheol* mean? Does it mean "hell" or does it mean merely "the grave"? Actually, it is used to refer to either or to both. Both Peter in his sermon at Pentecost and Paul in Antioch quote the Psalm as an Old Testament reference to the resurrection of Jesus, that his body was not to be left in Sheol or the grave.

The other passage not in 1 Peter is in Ephesians 4:8–9: " 'When He ascended on high, He led captives in His train and gave gifts to men.' What does 'He ascended' mean except that He also descended to the lower, earthly regions?" Now some interpreters take the words, "descended to the lower, earthly regions" to mean hades. But the two activities of Jesus that are compared in this passage are his ascension into heaven, and his descent, which seems to refer to his arrival on planet earth at his incarnation. Therefore many commentators on this passage refer to the descent here as Jesus' descent from heaven to earth; thus the reference to the ascension becomes the complement of the descent, or the completion of the round trip.

In 1 Peter 3:18–19 we read, "He [Jesus] was put to death in the body but made alive by the Spirit, through Whom also He went and preached to the spirits in prison who disobeyed long ago when God waited patiently in the days of Noah while the ark was being built." Please note that this discussion is really an aside; it is not the main point of the passage. Peter is referring to the power of the Holy Spirit, who raised Jesus from the dead, the same Spirit through whose power Jesus preached to those who long ago rebelled against God while Noah was building the ark. The ark was God's deliverance for Noah and his family from the judgment of the flood.

Now, when did the preaching take place? Some say it took place during the time of Noah, through the person of Noah. Others believe that Jesus preached righteousness to those persons who were in the prison of hell, but that he did it before they ever died, through the power of the Holy Spirit. Still others interpret this passage to mean that Jesus went to the prison of hell and preached to those held there who had died before and during the flood but who had never had a chance to hear God's word. By going to them he gave them a chance to believe. They were disembodied spirits being held in something like a spiritual Ellis Island until they were cleared.

Which is the right interpretation? Here again, we get a keyhole glimpse, which does not show us the whole picture. I am not sure that any one of these can be dogmatically referred to as *the* right interpretation.

The common Protestant interpretation of the passage is that in the Spirit, Christ preached through Noah to the disobedient who lived before the flood, who when Peter wrote were spirits in prison. But in 1 Peter 4:6 we find these words: "For this is the reason the gospel was preached even to those who are now dead, so that they might be judged according to men in regard to the body, but live according to God in regard to the spirit." When was the gospel preached to those who are now dead? Was it before they died or after they died?

Professor Louis Berkoff writes that the dead to whom the gospel was preached were evidently not yet dead when it was preached to them, because the purpose of the preaching was in part that they might be judged as living people. In such a case this could have taken place only during their lives on earth. In all probability Peter refers to the same spirits in prison of which he spoke in chapter 3.

Is there anything that can be said by way of summary of what this phrase means and how it is to be interpreted? The Roman Catholic church takes the phrase "He descended into hell" to mean that after his death, Christ went into Limbus Patrum, where the Old Testament saints were awaiting the revelation and application of his redemption. He preached the gospel to them, and then he brought them out and led them to heaven. The Lutherans regard the descent into Hades as the first stage of the exaltation of Christ. Christ went into the underworld to reveal, to consummate his victory over Satan and the powers of darkness, and to pronounce their sentence of

condemnation. Some Lutherans place this triumphal march between the death of Christ and his resurrection; others, after the
resurrection. The Church of England holds that while Christ's body
was in the grave his soul went into paradise, the abode of the souls of
the righteous, and there he gave them a fuller exposition of the
truth. John Calvin interprets the phrase metaphorically, as referring
to the penal sufferings of Christ on the cross, where he suffered the
pangs of hell while he was hanging there in our place.

Which interpretation is correct? I am not sure that it behooves us
to be dogmatic on any of them, but one thing I am sure of: that God
has left us with some degree of doubt on this matter in order to
impress upon us that God did much more for us through the death
of Jesus Christ than we have begun to realize or any one interpretation can grasp. We need to be open to the power of his salvation,
made available to us through the death of Jesus Christ.

What practical lesson can we draw from this? Let me suggest three
things. First, I would suggest that the phrase "He descended into
hell," and the passages of Scripture in Psalms, Ephesians, and
1 Peter that we have discussed all make clear one thing: that whatever hell is, and wherever it is, *we do not have to go there because Christ
has suffered our hell for us.* My friends, that is good news! If Jesus
Christ "bore our sins in his body on the tree, so that we might die to
sins and live for righteousness" (1 Peter 2:24), then the hell we
deserve in punishment for our sins has been endured by our Savior.
It behooves us to examine once again our own relationship with
him. Do we really trust him as our Savior? Do we really believe that
he died in our place on that cross? Do we really believe that he has
taken our hell for us?

The second lesson that we can learn from these passages of
Scripture—but particularly passages that refer to those who are dead
or are spirits in prison—is that *our God is just.* This preaching to the
spirits in prison was done through the power of the Spirit, either in
the days of Noah or during the death of Christ; but regardless of
which time, this preaching vindicates the justice of God. God does
not condemn people to hell unjustly. Whatever interpretation we
may place on that phrase about preaching to those who are dead or

who are spirits in prison, we have a glimpse through a keyhole not of the total truth, but enough of the truth to let us know that God does not condemn anyone to hell without a reason. In fact, the Scripture tells us clearly that "God is not willing that any should perish, but that all should come to repentance" (2 Peter 3:9). If that is what God wants, then a person goes to hell only because that person has jumped over a multitude of hurdles that God has erected to keep him or her from going there. Do not ever worry about anybody going to hell unjustly. Our question should be, Do we trust in him as our sovereign Lord?

Then finally, I believe that whatever else "descended into hell" means, and whatever else it teaches us, and whatever else we learn from this passage of Scripture before us, this is paramount: because sin put Jesus through the agony of hell, *we who trust him must turn our backs on the conduct, the ways of life, and the patterns of thought that put him there in our place.*

This is the appeal of Peter in chapter 4 of his epistle. After writing that Christ died and preached to the spirits in prison, he continues,

Therefore, since Christ suffered in his body, arm yourselves also with the same attitude, because he who has suffered in his body is done with sin. As a result, he does not live the rest of his earthly life for evil human desires, but rather for the will of God. For you have spent enough time in the past doing what pagans choose to do—living in debauchery, lust, drunkenness, orgies, carousing and detestable idolatry. They think it strange that you do not plunge with them into the same flood of dissipation, and they heap abuse on you. But they will have to give account to him who is ready to judge the living and the dead. For this is the reason the gospel was preached even to those who are now dead, so that they might be judged according to men in regard to the body, but live according to God in regard to the spirit. (1 Peter 1–6).

We do not do well if we take the Christian life lightly. God has called us to holiness. Being holy is nothing more than reflecting God's way of life in the world. Because sin is what put Christ on the cross and put him through the agony of hell, we as Christians must recommit our lives to reflecting his holiness and righteousness by the way we live.

Where was Jesus while his body was in the grave? We do not know for sure, but we do know that he who was crucified, dead, and buried *took our hell for us* so that we do not have to suffer the pangs of eternal death for ourselves. If he did that for us, what kind of people should we be as we live out the years of our lives?

Chapter 6

WHAT DOES EASTER HAVE TO DO WITH CHRISTMAS?

"And on the Third Day He Rose Again from the Dead"

Christmas is the biggest holiday of the American year. But its spiritual significance has become overshadowed by its commercial significance, and the Gift of God in Bethlehem's manger has been all but lost in wrap, ribbons, and reveling.

December 25 is a conjectural date for the birthday of Jesus. But whatever the true date, that day would have no meaning for us if it were not for the subsequent event that we celebrate on Easter. If there had been no Easter, there would be no celebration of Christmas.

If Jesus had not risen from the dead, why would we bother to remember his birth? If he had not risen from the dead he would have simply been a man whose claims of deity exhibited a megalomania which should have had him institutionalized. After all, the life of Jesus was not all that remarkable. The teachings of Jesus are ethically refreshing but without the truth of much that he taught being guaranteed by his resurrection, many of them are highly impractical.

Furthermore, if the writers who recorded his resurrection were not telling the truth, then can we believe anything else they wrote about Jesus' miracles? The death of Jesus was an obscure tragedy that was no more memorable than thousands of other crucifixions in barbaric Rome. We would not remember the birth of Jesus if he were still dead. The fact of Jesus' resurrection is the benchmark from which we measure everything else about Jesus Christ: his birth, his life, his teachings, his miracles, and even his death all derive their meaning from the fact that on "the third day he rose again from the dead."

In that statement there is one word that raises a question in some people's minds: that word is *again*. We often use that word to indicate a repetition of an act or an event. John got good grades *again*. Mary was late *again* to work. The president is going to run for office *again*. In each case we are referring to something that has happened before and now is recurring. If that was the only sense in which the word *again* could be used, it would indicate that the resurrection of Jesus was something that had happened at least once before.

But another way to use the word *again* is to use it to refer to a former condition. It is good to have Carolyn home *again*. What does that mean? It means that Carolyn was home and then she left home and now she is back. She has been restored to her former condition of residence in the home. Or George is conscious *again*. That means that George was conscious and then he went into a coma and now he has come out of the coma and once again is conscious. He has returned to a former condition of awareness.

When the creed affirms that Jesus rose again from the dead, it obviously is not referring to a repeat performance, but rather to the fact that Jesus returned to his former condition of life after being dead.

What does it mean when we say, "On the third day he rose again from the dead"? What is contained in this article of faith in the Creed? I want us to consider three things that we are affirming when we say, "On the third day He rose again from the dead." First, let's look at the fact of Jesus' resurrection. Second, we'll look at the form of Jesus' resurrection. Finally, we will look at the faith that flows out of, or follows from, Jesus' resurrection.

First, let us look at the fact of Jesus' resurrection. How do we know that Jesus rose from the dead? There are several lines of evidence, and the first line is that of testimony. For testimony to be believable, it has to come from credible witnesses, and there are at least three things necessary for a witness to be credible. First, the witness must be competent. In most cases that means that he or she must be an eyewitness to that of which he or she bears testimony. Second, for a testimony to be believed, particularly if it is about something out of the realm of ordinary experience, there must be sufficient numbers. (In looking for the evidence of UFOs we find a lot of individual testimonies to their existence, but no evidence that comes from a large number of people all seeing the same thing in the same way. There must be a sufficient number of people with the same testimony.) Finally, a witness must have a good reputation. In all three of these areas the disciples qualify. Repeatedly they claimed to be eyewitnesses to the resurrection. Furthermore, more than five hundred at one time saw the risen Lord. And no one has ever attacked the moral or ethical character of the eyewitnesses. People who do not believe in the resurrection do not say the disciples were dishonest people. At the worst they simply say that the disciples were deluded. But the disciples could have had no ulterior motive for affirming Jesus' resurrection, because they did so at the risk of their lives; knowing this we can understand that they were telling the truth.

Another line of evidence that we can examine regarding the fact of Jesus' resurrection is that of cause and effect. Every effect has a cause, and there are a number of effects that must be traced to the resurrection of Jesus as their cause. The first effect is that of the empty tomb. Where was the body? The Jewish authorities started the rumor that the disciples had stolen it (Matt. 28:11–15). But why would they leave the grave clothes lying there as though the material body had evaporated through them? Furthermore, if the disciples stole the body, why would they die for an untruth? The essence of their preaching hinged upon the truth of the resurrection: why would they be willing to be put to death because of a hoax? And if the disciples stole the body away, how could so many have remained true to a hoax? If you have read about major crimes committed by a group of people, you know that the larger the group of people involved in the crime, the greater the chance of solving the crime because sooner or later somebody is likely to break. Whether it is a great train robbery, or a bank robbery or what have you, the more people involved in it, the more likelihood that sooner or later somebody is going to step forward and say, "This is what really happened." There were many individual witnesses who saw the risen Lord. There were several small groups who met with Him. On one occasion there were over five hundred at one time who saw the risen Lord. With this kind of evidence, that early church, to a person, was prepared to die for their faith which was based on the reality of the resurrection of Jesus.

Some people say that officials stole the body of Jesus in order to keep the disciples from doing the same thing. By securing the body of Jesus, they would frustrate the plans of the disciples to perpetrate a hoax. That is absurd. If the officials had stolen the body so as to stop the preaching of the disciples and the growth of that early church, they would have then simply produced the body, because the preaching of that early church centered on the resurrection. That was the greatest thing that had happened, and the disciples announced it to the world. It was the greatest evidence of the power of God at work in human life. So the officials could simply have produced the body and said, "Here it is. Now stop preaching." But they did not because they could not.

Another effect that owes its cause to the resurrection of Jesus is something often overlooked: the Lord's Day. Sunday as a day of worship replaced the Sabbath because the early church, although steeped in Judaism, remembered Sunday as the day of resurrection, the first day of the week, not the seventh day. The reason we observe this first day of the week as the primary day of worship is because it is the day on which Jesus Christ rose from the dead. Every Sunday is a commemoration of the resurrection. Historically, why would a faith that had its roots in Judaism have changed its holy day from Saturday to Sunday if it were not for the fact that Sunday was understood to be the day of resurrection?

A third effect that owes its cause to the resurrection is the existence of the Christian church itself. As great as was the impression made upon the disciples by the life of Jesus, all of their hopes were dashed, utterly dashed, when Jesus was crucified. They had lived and walked with him for three years. They heard him speak. They had watched him perform miracles. They had had great hopes and expectations, and they were there when he was nailed to that cross. They were utterly downfallen when Jesus was laid in the tomb. What changed the disciples? What produced that miraculous turnaround in their attitude that made them people who were bold enough to go into the world and preach about Jesus Christ? It was the assurance of the resurrection! On the basis of that which changed the disciples, they then went out to tell the Good News of God's work in Christ, and the Good News of the resurrection, and from those beginnings arose the Christian church. The church would not exist if Christ had not risen from the dead.

A fourth effect of the truth of the resurrection is the New Testament itself. The twenty-nine books that we call the New Testament were written for the purpose of communicating the Good News of the life and death and resurrection of Jesus Christ; and to instruct early gatherings of believers in such places as Philippi, Corinth, and Ephesus how they were to live in the light of the resurrection of Jesus Christ. We would not have a New Testament if Jesus had not risen. Who would have written about a man who had failed in the greatest claim that he made about himself, that he could defeat the enemy that frightens us all: death?

So the fact of the resurrection has good evidence to underscore its reality.

Let us now examine the form of the resurrection, in specific, three things.

First, the resurrection of Jesus was a real resurrection. It was not a resuscitation from a swoon or a faint. Some people have said that Jesus really did not die. From loss of blood, pain, and the shock of the crucifixion, he simply went into a deep swoon or a faint, and while he was lying in that cool grave, he gradually regained consciousness. But nothing about the death and burial of Jesus Christ lends credence to that notion. The effects of a crucifixion are excruciatingly painful and traumatic. A crucified person gradually bleeds to death, while nailed to a cross. Then the cross is picked up and dropped into a hole. Every major joint in the body is dislocated. If you have ever experienced the pain of a dislocated thumb or a dislocated shoulder you know that dislocated joints do not recover their strength very quickly. How much more painful, and how much weaker would be the person who experienced the dislocation of most of the major joints of the body. Combine that weakness with the loss of blood, and the inanity of the swoon theory is obvious. There is no way that Jesus, after a short time in the grave, could have recovered his consciousness and then physically rolled that stone away, especially from the inside. Several strong able-bodied women went to the grave, and they said, "Who is going to roll away the stone for us, for it is too large" (Mark 16:3). If they could not have done it from the outside, a person who had gone through the agony of crucifixion certainly could not have done it from the inside. Furthermore, the centurion and the soldiers looked at Jesus and they said he was dead. They had seen the loss of blood; they had seen his side pierced by a spear, and water spurt from that wound. They were familiar with death by crucifixion, and they knew that he was dead. The people who took him down from the cross and the women who wrapped his body in those grave clothes knew that he was dead. Then they went to the grave on that first day of the week in the expectation of anointing a dead body. And Christ himself declared to John that he had been dead and now was alive forevermore (Rev. 1:18).

Second, the resurrection of Jesus was a bodily resurrection. Some people who claim to believe in the resurrection of Jesus Christ have difficulty with the idea of the resurrection of the body as opposed to a resurrection of the spirit of Jesus. Jehovah's Witnesses, Christian Scientists, and liberal Protestants hold to this latter interpretation in various forms. But Jesus himself declared after his resurrection, "A spirit does not have flesh and blood as you see Me have" (Luke 24:39). Matthew said that the women who met Jesus on the resurrection morning held him by the feet. Furthermore, his body was recognized after the resurrection, even down to the nail wounds in his hands. And in the presence of his disciples after he had risen,

Jesus ate food. So the resurrection of Jesus was a bodily resurrection. Finally, the resurrection of Jesus was a unique resurrection. It was different from all other resurrections recorded in Scripture. Yes, it was a real body. It was recognized as the same body. It had flesh and blood. It could be, and was, touched. Yet in mysterious ways it was different after the resurrection, for he could pass through closed doors, could move about without reference to time or space, and did not have to have food or sleep; and he is now alive forevermore. I will say more about this when we come to that phrase in the Creed that talks about the body and the life everlasting, for how do we know what our resurrection bodies will be like except as we view what happened to Jesus Christ. As one lady said to me several years ago, and the older I get the more I can understand and agree with her viewpoint, "When the Lord raises my body from the dead, I hope he does something to it and that it is different than it is now." I believe the Bible teaches us that is the case.

Let us now consider the faith that follows the resurrection of Jesus, for it is the resurrection of Jesus that attests to his true deity. It is his resurrection that assures us that all that he said about himself, and all that he said about life, and all that he taught us about heaven are really true. The resurrection also assures us of the adequacy of Jesus' work for our atonement. We would not know that Jesus' death was powerful enough to save us if he had not risen from the dead.

The last stanza of "O Sing a Song of Bethlehem," written by Louis F. Benson in 1899 reads

> Oh, sing a song of Calvary, its glory and dismay.
> Of Him Who hung upon the tree and took our sins away.
> For He Who died on Calvary is risen from the grave,
> and Christ, our Lord, by heaven adored, is mighty now to save.

That is the affirmation of the resurrection to us. It is the guarantee of our faith that what we believe about forgiveness and the atonement, as well as what we believe about heaven and eternal life, are guaranteed by the resurrection.

Furthermore, the resurrection makes possible the continued work of Christ for us as our High Priest, our Intercessor, and our Protector. I will say more about this in chapter 7.

Finally, the resurrection is the basis for our assurance that all of the necessary power of God is available to us as we try to live this life as followers of Jesus Christ, and as we live this life in preparation for the life to come. The Good News that came to us through the person we call Jesus Christ came into this world through the womb of Mary, a virgin; but his mission was not completed until his final victory over sin and Satan when, on the third day, he rose again from the dead. That, my reader friend, is the only basis for celebrating Christmas—or for that matter, for celebrating anything else about Jesus Christ, our Lord.

Chapter 7

WHAT IS JESUS DOING NOW?

"He Ascended into Heaven, and Sitteth on the Right Hand of God the Father Almighty."

If Jesus rose from the dead, where is he now and what is he doing now?

Jesus' life and ministry took place on earth nearly two thousand years ago. That is ancient history. Is that all there is to Christianity: the discussion of his life, death, and resurrection?

It is indeed "Good News" that Jesus died for our sins and rose from the dead as victor over death, hell, and the grave. But often, in living out this faith in a hostile world where the enemy is not just out there but inside our very beings, it would be nice to know Jesus had some help to offer now, in this struggle. Is the salvation he offers only for when we die? Or can he give us help now?

But what does it mean for Christ to be our Savior? How does he go about saving us?

Sometimes we turn away from something that is old because we think that, because of its age, it has become outmoded. There must be a more modern, and therefore better, way. Occasionally we find, usually to our chagrin, that there are some old ways that really can't be improved upon. The Westminster Shorter Catechism falls into this category. It contains, in question-and-answer format, a magnificent statement of faith that will bring an immeasurable stability to your faith and life and conduct. I was forced to memorize the Shorter Catechism at an early age, and hated every minute of it. But in later years I discovered that the truths that were embedded in my mind surfaced often to give support in time of doubt or trouble. To be sure, I would modernize the King James' English of the document, but the systematic body of doctrine I would alter not at all. What a source of strength it has been for me.

Question number 23 of the Westminster Shorter Catechism asks, "What offices does Christ execute as our Redeemer?" If I were writing a modern revision of that question and its answer I would ask, "What functions does Christ carry out as our Savior?" The answer would be, "Christ, as our Savior, carries out the functions of a prophet, a priest, and of a King, both in His condition of humiliation and exaltation."

Thus far in our consideration of the Apostles' Creed we have seen what it means to affirm faith in God the Father almighty, maker of heaven and Earth, and we also have considered what it means to affirm faith in Jesus Christ as the Son of God, born of a virgin through the conceiving agency of the Holy Spirit; and we have examined the suffering life and death of Jesus, and sought to understand better what it means to believe in the resurrection. Now we come to a phrase about which some people have asked, "Why is it even in the creed? I do not understand its importance." The phrase is, "He ascended into heaven, and sitteth on the right hand of God the Father almighty."

Why is a reference to the ascension of Jesus in the Creed? And if it is important to have it in there, what is Jesus doing now?

In the mid 1960s Bishop John A. T. Robinson of the Anglican church wrote a book entitled *Honest to God,* which was greeted with acclaim by some and criticized by others. Bishop Robinson objects to the notion that God is *up* there somewhere, because he feels that modern cosmology has done away with the possibility that heaven is up and hell is down and we are living in a middle tier of a three-story universe. I think that Bishop Robinson and others who object to the doctrine of the ascension on the basis of Copernican cosmology miss the point altogether. The ascension of Jesus was a complement to the Incarnation. The Incarnation refers to God taking on human flesh in the Person that we know as his Son, Jesus. Jesus' Incarnation was the descent from God to man, from man to poverty, from poverty to a criminal's death. The ascension was a reversal of that process. It was his return to his former condition of life with the Father.

There are many references to the ascension in the New Testament. Only Luke mentions the event itself, in the end of his Gospel and in the beginning of the book of Acts. Let us look at these references while pondering what the creed means when it says, "He ascended into heaven, and sitteth on the right hand of God the Father almighty."

The first reference is in Luke 24:50–53:

When He had led them out to the vicinity of Bethany, He lifted up his hands and blessed them. While He was blessing them, He left them and was taken up into heaven. Then they worshiped him, and returned to Jerusalem with great joy. And they stayed continually at the temple, praising God.

In Acts 1:6–9 we read

So when they met together, they asked him, "Lord, are you at this time going to restore the kingdom to Israel?" He said to them, "It is not for you to know the times or dates the Father has set by his own authority. But you will receive power when the Holy Spirit comes on you; and you will be my witnesses in Jerusalem, and in all Judea and Samaria, and to the ends of the earth." After he said this, he was taken up before their very eyes, and a cloud hid him from their sight.

In the Gospel of John 14:2 and 12, Jesus is speaking to his disciples:

In my Father's house are many rooms; if it were not so, I would have told you. I am going there to prepare a place for you. . . . I tell you the truth, anyone who has faith in me will do what I have been doing. He will do even greater things than these, because I am going to the Father.

In John 16:5:

Now I am going to Him who sent me.

And in verse 10 he says,

I am going to the Father.

Again, in John 16:28:

I came from the Father, and entered the world; now I am leaving the world and going back to the Father.

John 17 is called the high priestly prayer of our Lord, In verse 5, speaking to his heavenly Father, Jesus says,

And now, Father, glorify me in your presence with the glory I had with you before the world began.

When Jesus appears in the Garden of Gethsemane to Mary after the resurrection, she grabs him by the feet. Jesus says to her,

Do not hold onto me for I have not yet returned to the Father. Go instead to my brothers and tell them, "I am returning to my Father and your Father, to My God and your God" (John 20:17).

The Apostle Paul in writing to the Ephesian Christians refers to what God has done for us,

which He accomplished in Christ when He raised Him from the dead and made Him sit at His right hand in the heavenly places (Eph. 1:20).

Again, Paul writes to Timothy:

Great indeed we confess is the mystery of our religion. He was manifested in the flesh, vindicated in the Spirit, seen by angels, preached among the nations, believed on in the world, taken up in glory (1 Tim. 3:16).

The book of Hebrews offers some of the most comprehensive pictures of Jesus' present place and ministry:

He reflects the glory of God and bears the very stamp of His nature upholding the universe by His word of power. When He had made purification for sins, He sat down at the right hand of the Majesty on High (Heb. 1:3).

Since then we have a great High Priest Who has passed through the heavens, Jesus the Son of God, let us hold fast our confession (Heb. 4:14).

Then

For Christ has entered, not into a sanctuary made with hands, a copy of the true one, but into heaven itself, now to appear in the presence of God on our behalf (Heb. 9:24).

Now there have been many of those priests, since death prevented them from continuing in office; but because Jesus lives forever, he has a permanent priesthood. Therefore he is able to save completely those who come to

God through him, because he always lives to intercede for them. Such a high priest meets our need—one who is holy, blameless, pure, set apart from sinners, exalted above the heavens. Unlike the other high priests, he does not need to offer sacrifices day after day, first for his own sins, and then for the sins of the people. He sacrificed for their sins once for all when he offered himself. For the law appoints as high priests men who are weak; but the oath, which came after the law, appointed the Son, who has been made perfect forever. The point of what we are saying is this: We do have such a high priest, who sat down at the right hand of the throne of the Majesty in heaven. (Heb. 7:23–8:1).

What picture do we get from all these references to the ascension of Jesus Christ?

The ascent means a return to his former place with the Father. What difference is it where that is, whether it is "up there" or "out there?" One objection to the idea that the ascent of Christ means "going up" to the Father is that if he went up to the Father, then he had to ascend to heaven. If a person has to go up to heaven, then those who live on the opposite side of the earth from wherever heaven is have to go right through the heart of the earth to get there. How ridiculous! Jesus' return to his former place with the Father is not to a place in our physical universe with material dimensions. Heaven is outside of our material and temporal dimension, and to return to that dimension is an elevation to a better dimension. So what better way for Jesus to return to that dimension than to be lifted up bodily, in the presence of the disciples, from their presence and to have a cloud hide him from their view. They knew that he was alive, but that he had moved into the presence of God.

It is noteworthy that when Luke refers to the ascension in the Gospel, he says that when Jesus left the disciples, they went back into the city *with great joy*. Imagine what would have happened if Jesus had walked out of a room, closed the door, and had never seen anything of them again. They would have wondered, What has happened to him? Where is he? But it was the visible, physical ascent that gave them the reassurance that he was alive, he was available to them, he just was not physically present. When we say that he ascended into heaven and sits on the right hand of God the Father almighty, that is simply a way of saying that he has taken a place of honor and authority in the presence of his Father.

If Jesus has ascended into heaven, what is he doing now? In the Westminster Shorter Catechism, we are told that Jesus executes his office of Savior by being a Prophet, a Priest, and a King. The catechism goes on in succeeding questions and answers to say that he performs the role of a Prophet in revealing to us by his Word and Spirit the will of God for our salvation. Jesus Christ is continuing to do that through everyone who proclaims his word; by the power of his Spirit, he informs all the world that God has a plan for their salvation. Whether it is the preacher in the pulpit, or the Sunday School teacher behind the lectern, or someone sharing with a neighbor the Good News of God's love and salvation provided in Jesus Christ, that is Christ at work in and through that person through his Word and by his Spirit. Furthermore, Jesus Christ continues to carry out the role of a Priest by offering himself once as sacrifice for sin to satisfy divine justice and to reconcile us to God, and now in interceding for us. Christ is praying for us. He is continuing to do that. Then Christ carries out the role of a King in first subduing us to himself, in ruling and defending us, and in restraining and conquering all his enemies and ours.

What is Jesus Christ doing now, and what does this mean for Christians living in this twentieth century?

Four things come to mind.

First, the ascended Lord Jesus Christ is our Advocate. He is our Defense Attorney before the Father in heaven. This is the meaning of John's words in 1 John 2:1: "But if anybody does sin, we have One Who speaks to the Father in our defense, Jesus Christ, the Righteous One." Christians struggle continually with a sense of guilt. If a person has confessed sin to God, and still feels guilty, let me say why: it is because that person has not understood that when sin is confessed, God forgives. We have a Defense Attorney before the Father. The Bible tells us that our great enemy, the devil, is our accuser. He constantly is badmouthing us to God. He also badmouths us to ourselves. Jesus Christ is our Advocate, our Defense Attorney. This is why Paul writes, "If anyone is in Christ, he is a new creation" (2 Cor. 5:17). And "there is now therefore no condemnation [no guilt] to those who are in Christ" (Rom. 8:1). That is Good News! If you are suffering from guilt and you do not know why, it may be because you have not recognized this marvelous truth: Christ is your Defense Attorney.

Another thing that the ascended Lord Jesus Christ does is to act as our Advance Agent. Jesus put it this way in John 14:3: "If I go and prepare a place for you, I will come back and take you to be with me that you also may be where I am." Wherever heaven is, Christ is there, and he is getting it ready for us.

Also, the ascended Lord Jesus Christ is our Intercessor. He is still our Priest. He is still the One who prays for us, even when we do not know how to pray for ourselves. What a wonderful reality it was that broke upon my own mind early in my life when I realized that Jesus Christ was praying for me. I remember the words of Jesus to Peter when Jesus knew that Peter was facing that dire temptation to turn his back on Jesus, to renounce and disown him. Jesus said to Peter, "Peter, I have prayed for you that your faith fail not" (Luke 22:32). My friends, he is doing that for each of us.

Then finally, the ascended Lord Jesus Christ is the Authority, the Ruler over the church, and he is the Sovereign over history. Christ, who died on a cross to pay the penalty for our sins, and who rose again from the dead, triumphant over sin and the grave, is the One who has won the battle against sin. He is the One who assures us that because he has conquered sin, we too shall see that time when sin is defeated in our own lives.

So Christ is busy for us. It is with joy that we can affirm, "He ascended into heaven, and sitteth on the right hand of God the Father almighty."

Chapter 8

THE SEQUEL TO CHRISTMAS

"From Thence He Shall Come To Judge the Quick and the Dead."

The world has not seen the last of Jesus Christ. He who came into this world and whose birth we celebrate at Christmas has something else to do.

Thus far we have seen that the Apostles' Creed affirms that Jesus Christ is the only Son of God the Father. He is our Lord. He entered this world by being conceived through the power of the Holy Spirit and in the womb of Mary, a virgin. He suffered and died during the rule of, and at the hand of, a ruler named Pontius Pilate. He was raised from the dead. He passed into the presence of God the Father, where currently he occupies a place of honor and authority.

But Jesus Christ is not through with this world yet. "From thence he shall come to judge the quick and the dead" makes two simple affirmations. The first affirmation is that Jesus is coming again. The second affirmation is that all people will give a final accounting to him. The first affirmation is an affirmation of hope; the second an affirmation of responsibility.

The second coming of Christ is the sequel to Christmas. There are numerous references in the Bible to the return of Jesus. To establish some Biblical basis for the teaching about the fact of the second coming, let me refer to some of these verses of Scripture.

In John 14:3 Jesus says to his disciples,

And if I go and prepare a place for you, I will come back and take you to be with me that you also may be where I am.

Hebrews 9:27:

So Christ having been offered once to bear the sins of many will appear a second time.

Philippians 3:20–21:

But our citizenship is in heaven, and from it we await a Savior, the Lord Jesus Christ, Who will change our lowly body to be like His glorious body by the power which enables Him even to subject all things to Himself.

Acts 3:19–21:

Repent, therefore, and turn again that your sins may be blotted out. That times of refreshing may come from the presence of the Lord, and that He may send the Christ appointed for you, Jesus, Whom the heavens must receive until the time for establishing all that God spoke by the mouth of His holy prophets from of old.

And those familiar words from Acts 1:9–11:

When Jesus had said this, as they were looking on, He was lifted up. And a cloud took Him out of their sight. While they were gazing into heaven as He went, behold, two men stood by them in white robes and said, "Men of Galilee, why do you stand looking into heaven? This Jesus Who was taken up from you into heaven will come in the same way as you saw Him go into heaven."

In 1 Thessalonians 4:15–17, Paul writes:

According to the Lord's own word, we tell you that we who are still alive, who are left till the coming of the Lord, will certainly not precede those who have fallen asleep. For the Lord himself will come down from heaven, with a loud command, with the voice of the archangel and with the trumpet call of God, and the dead in Christ will rise first. After that, we who are still alive and are left will be caught up together with them in the clouds to meet the Lord in the air. And so we will be with the Lord forever.

These are but a few of the references in the Bible to the clear affirmation that Jesus Christ will come again. But some people have a hard time with the idea of a literal, bodily, visible return of Jesus Christ to the Earth. That should not surprise us. In the days of Jesus' life, people had a hard time understanding how Jesus Christ could be the Messiah and literally fulfill the prophecies of the Old Testament.

There are several alternate ways of interpreting the passages concerning the second coming.

One interpretation is that Jesus comes again at the death of every believer. There is, of course, truth in that. When a person dies the Lord has come to that person and called him or her into his nearer presence. When a believer dies, the Lord is indeed coming for him or her. But when Jesus comes for an individual believer, it does not satisfy all that the Scripture has to say about what will happen at the return of Christ. For Jesus does not come with a shout and the sound of a trumpet, and every eye does not behold him every time a believer dies.

Another interpretation of the second coming is to equate it with the coming of the Holy Spirit at Pentecost. Again, there is truth in this, for Jesus did say to his disciples, "I will not leave you comfortless. I will come to you" (John 14:18). He was talking specifically about the fact that he was going to send the Comforter, the Paraclete (which means "the One called alongside of us"), as an encourager, a guide, and a help. When Jesus sent the Holy Spirit to his disciples, in a very real sense that was his coming alongside of them. But here again, it does not fulfill all of the conditions that are mentioned in the preceeding references concerning the return of Christ.

A third interpretation of Jesus' return sees his promise as fulfilled with the destruction of Jerusalem in A.D. 70. The disciples pointed out to Jesus the magnificent structure of the temple. Jesus responded by saying, "As for what you see here, the time will come when not one stone will be left on another."

"When will these things happen?" they asked. "What will be the sign that they are about to take place" (Luke 21:6ff).

Then Jesus prophesied about events in the future that would precede his return. His answer seemed to cover many events, of which the destruction of Jerusalem in A.D. 70 was only the first. Jesus told that the destruction of the temple was coming as an act of judgment by God upon that city. The disciples asked for signs that would lead up to it. Jesus gave them signs that would precede that final great judgment, which would be initiated by his return.

So divine judgment is one aspect of Christ returning, and thus the destruction of Jerusalem partially fulfilled his prophecy about coming again. Yet the dead in Christ did not rise. Living believers were not caught up in the air to be with Christ. The bodies of believers were not transformed. So, although there was a coming of Christ in judgment in A.D. 70 on that city, still that event did not fulfill all of the conditions that the Scripture says will occur when Christ comes again.

Furthermore, years after the destruction of Jerusalem, the Apostle John, in the book of Revelation, is still looking forward to the Lord's coming.

So the Scripture teaches plainly that Jesus Christ is going to come again, and that that prophecy has not yet been completely fulfilled. It is still to come. The world has not seen the last of Jesus Christ. His coming again will be the sequel to Christmas.

A tragedy of the church's history is that some people try to learn more than God wants them to know. Just before the ascension, when Jesus returned to the Father, the disciples asked him, "Lord, are you at this time going to restore the kingdom to Israel?"

Jesus replied, "It is not for you to know the times or dates the Father has set by his own authority." But from that time to the present, Christians have persisted in trying to set dates or perhaps outlines of schedules regarding Jesus' return. Some have even compiled detailed charts for the second coming. I have seen churches split over questions of how he is going to come, when he is going to come, and what is going to happen after he comes. Such concern diverts Christians from the main purpose for which he leaves us here. This is made plain by Jesus when he says, "You will receive power when the Holy Spirit comes on you; and you will be my witnesses" (Acts 1:8).

Christ is going to come again. We affirm that every time we say the Apostles' Creed.

But when he comes again, what will he do? He will come as judge: "From thence he shall come to judge the quick and the dead."

Jesus says, "The Father judges no one, but has entrusted all judgment to the Son" (John 5:22). In Acts 10 Paul says, "He is the One
Who God appointed as judge of the living and of the dead."

What are we affirming when we say that he will judge the quick
and the dead? The word *quick* is derived from an Old English word,
cwic, meaning "alive." So this reference is to those who are alive at
the time of Jesus' return as well as those who have died prior to his
return. Everyone must stand before the judgment seat of Christ. If
we are all going to stand before the judgment seat of Christ, if when
he comes again we all appear before him to give accountings of our
lives, then what will be the basis for judgment?

When we stand before the Lord as Judge, he will judge us on the
basis of reality as he knows it, and not appearances as we see it. We
humans judge on the basis of appearances. We try to get at the facts,
but even when judges and lawyers and juries do their very best, they
sometimes make mistakes because not all of the facts are known.
One person sees another do something or say something, and the
first person jumps to a wrong conclusion. This erroneous conclusion leads that person to make a wrong judgment, and the other
person is consequently hurt by it.

But when the Lord judges us, he will be totally fair. Not only will
he judge us on the basis of all the facts, he will also judge us on the
basis of what he knows to be our motives and our intentions. God is
absolutely righteous and absolutely just: we need not fear that he
will make a mistake in his evaluation of us.

Another thing to understand about the judgment of Christ is that
the judgment he renders will be eternal justice according to God's
laws, and not human justice based on human-made laws. Every
counselor, whether minister, psychiatrist, or psychologist, knows
that one of the major problems in counseling is dealing with guilt.
We also know that there are two different kinds of guilt. There is
real guilt when a person has genuinely failed to live up to the
legitimate, realistic standard of God's expectation. When the Scripture says we have sinned and come short of the glory of God (Rom.
3:23), it is affirming that we have failed to live up to God's standard,
and therefore are guilty before him. But the Scripture also tells us

how to deal with that. The Bible tells us in 1 John 1:9 that if we sin, we are to confess our sin to God, the One who is faithful and just, so that he will forgive us our sin and cleanse us from all unrighteousness. Real guilt can be dealt with by confessing the sin and accepting the forgiveness that God offers. If we have sinned against someone else, then we must confess our sin to him or her and ask for forgiveness.

The more tenacious problem with which we must deal is false guilt, or a guilt complex. A person may have been raised with an unrealistic standard imposed upon him by parents or peers or community. Such a person feels that he or she always fall short, never can meet expectations. This person has imposed upon himself or herself such unrealistic standards that the person lives with a continual sense of failure.

But when Jesus judges us, his judgment will be rendered on the basis of God's laws, full knowledge of all the facts, and a true understanding of the motivations of our hearts.

Yet another thing to comprehend about this judgment of Christ is that we will be judged on the basis of our acceptance of God's love by faith, and not the earning of God's love and approval by good works. Theoretically there are two ways of attaining righteousness, a right standing before God. One is by keeping all the demands of God, known as the law. That means being perfect. But the Bible says in Romans 8:23 that "all have sinned and fall short of the glory of God." Those who try to attain righteousness by fully upholding the law are doomed to failure. No one can live by God's perfect standard.

So to give us access to his presence, God has given us another way: the righteousness of Christ, which becomes our righteousness by faith in what Jesus Christ has done for us. That is what the book of Romans is about: how we can achieve the righteousness of God. God is not willing that any should perish, but that all should come to repentance, and God has provided a way for us to have access to his presence, to stand before him and be a member of his family. He has made it possible for us to be righteous, but it comes by faith, not by works. So the judgment that Christ will render will be based upon our righteousness by faith, and not upon our righteousness through our good works, for we cannot attain righteousness that way.

For those who do not accept the righteousness that God offers to us in Jesus Christ by faith, there is nothing else left but for God to take his loving hands from us and give us what we want, which is absence from him. It was Professor Chad Walsh who wrote that, "Hell is God's last gift of love to those who will accept nothing else from His hands." He wants to give us life. He wants to give us forgiveness. He wants to give us his righteousness. He wants to give us heaven. When we refuse what he offers on his terms, there is nothing else left but to give us what we want on our terms. That is hell.

Finally, the judgment of Christ is going to be based on obedience to Christ in faith and not faith as an empty profession. Faith always shows itself in the way we act. The way we act is always a revelation of what we really believe. So obedience that has its roots in faith in Jesus Christ is the foundation for the living of a godly life. It is not words of faith. Jesus Christ is able to distinguish between the faith that produces good works, and the faith that is an empty profession.

Where does the believer stand in all of this? When we stand before the Judge, if we have known the Judge as our Savior, if we have trusted him as our Lord, there is no fear. Paul puts it this way: "There is therefore now no condemnation to those who are in Christ Jesus" Rom. 8:1. The appearance of Christ holds no fear for those who trust him, those who love him, those who obey him. For the Judge is also our Defense Attorney. He is our Advocate.

What are the practical implications of affirming "From thence he shall come to judge the quick and the dead"? There are at least three.

The first implication I see for this affirmation that Jesus Christ is going to come again to judge us is that the return of Jesus Christ as Judge will fulfill two deep longings of humanity, longings that are built into every human heart and soul. One is the longing for justice. In a world where injustice is a part of being human, where injustice exists because as human beings we are incapable of total justice, the coming of Christ will satisfy that longing for justice. There is only One who will render perfect justice. So where there is unfairness, we can be assured that there is One who is going to come to set that right, satisfying one of the deep longings of the human heart.

The other longing is for fulfillment and restoration. In looking at the world around us, we know that something has distorted the plan. Personal relationships can break; nature itself can become our enemy. Millions have died in African famines; many have been killed by volcanoes, tidal waves, hurricanes, and earthquakes. They indicate that the world somehow is at war with itself. The Apostle Paul puts it this way: "For the creation was subjected to frustration, not by its own choice, but by the will of the One who subjected it, in hope that the creation itself will be liberated from its bondage to decay and brought into the glorious freedom of the children of God" Rom. 8:20–21. The time toward which even creation is looking to correct the damage and distortion of the effects of sin is the time of the coming of Christ, when a new heaven and a new earth will be created.

Do not ask me what this new heaven and new earth will look like. I do not know. All I know is that you can let your imagination run wild, because the Scripture says that the best is yet to be. We cannot even imagine the good things that God has prepared for those who love him. So whatever it is, it is desirable, it is worthwhile, and it will come to pass because Jesus Christ will come again.

So the return of Christ as Judge will fulfill these two deep longings of humanity. God will set things right and God will make things perfect.

Also, the second coming of Jesus Christ is the basis for mutual encouragement. In 1 Thessalonians 4:13–18, the Apostle Paul begins by saying, "But we would not have you to be ignorant, brethren, concerning those who are asleep, that you sorrow not as others who don't have any hope." He goes on to talk about how those who have died are in Christ's presence. Then he says, after affirming the return of Christ, "Therefore, comfort [the Greek word used here means 'encouragement'] one another with these words." Many have stood by the open graves of loved ones who have been seen on this earth for the last time. Some have suffered because of disease. Some have suffered because of accidents. They have seen the suffering in the world. The word of God says to encourage one another with the reality of Jesus' return. These words about the return of Jesus Christ are important to all of us. If we do not believe them, then where are we headed?

Finally, the hope of Christ's return is the great biblical argument for a godly life. Matthew 24:44–51, Luke 21:34–36, and 1 John 2:18 are three passages of a number that tell us that because Christ is going to come, a believer must be watchful, faithful, wise, and obedient; and live a life of simplicity, self-control, and prayer. This is because the believer does not want to be embarrassed when the Master comes back again. Do not get caught short. Be alert. We do not know when it is going to happen. But be ready.

So we are encouraged to a life of godliness because we believe that Christ is going to come again as the Judge of the quick and the dead. Maybe tomorrow!

Chapter 9

GOD IN THE PRESENT TENSE

"I Believe in the Holy Ghost"

Has your conscience ever bothered you because you had done something wrong? Had you then been led to confess that sin and experience the gracious cleanness that comes from knowing you have been forgiven? If you have, then you have experienced something of the presence and the power of the Holy Spirit.

Have you ever gone through a time of great turmoil, fear, or grief, and then, in your concern turned to God, and found your life flooded with a deep sense of peace that no one else could understand? It is a peace that comes from knowing that God is in control and your life is in his hands. If you have, you know something about the work of the Holy Spirit.

Can you remember back to that time when you first became convinced that Jesus Christ is the Son of God and your Savior from sin? It may have come after years of being raised in a Christian family and the nurture of the church, and then one day you claimed for yourself that which you had been taught since early childhood. As a young person the truth dawned upon you. Or maybe you grew up outside the church but somewhere you heard the Good News that God loves you and gave his Son for you, and you were convinced of the truth of that message. You opened your heart to him and experienced the wonder of conversion. If you are a believer in Jesus Christ and are convinced of the truth of the gospel, you have experienced something of the power and the love and the grace of the Holy Spirit.

The disciples were good Jews, familiar with Old Testament history and faith. They knew a God whom they called Jehovah through the testimony of Moses and the prophets, as well as the old traditions that had been handed down from one generation to another. Jehovah was the God who created, the God who had made a covenant with Abraham, the God who judged his people for their sins and failures, and the God who had promised renewal and restoration to his people. The disciples had also discovered that the ancient God of past history has a Son and his name is Jesus and that Jesus is Immanuel, "God with us."

These disciples had experienced and had come to believe that the invisible God above them is made visible by God among them, and that his name is Jesus. Everything that they needed to know about Jehovah was to be learned in Jesus of Nazareth. But beyond cognitive knowledge of God they discovered that in Jesus Christ, the invisible Inhabiter of eternity had become their Savior, and the Savior of all who would believe in him, by dying for them on a cross. These disciples had seen Jesus crucified. On the third day they had seen him alive, resurrected. They had fellowship with him. Then they had seen him ascend into heaven. Before he left, Jesus had promised that he would not leave them alone. Yet there they were. Jesus had gone. Now they wondered, How will we experience his presence?

Jesus had already told them. Yet they still were not sure. They did not know, for they had experienced the God who was above them; they had known the God who was among them; but then at Pentecost they were to receive the God who would be within them. So from that day to this, part of the church's faith has been to affirm, "I believe in the Holy Ghost." The word *ghost* is an old way of referring to a spirit who has personality and existence independent from a physical body. Maybe one of these days we will get around to replacing the word 'ghost' with the word 'spirit', for it would make much more sense to our modern generation.

The affirmation in the creed is short: "I believe in the Holy Ghost." Why do we have such a brief affirmation about the Holy Spirit? The Apostles' Creed starts with a short affirmation about God the Father almighty, maker of heaven and earth. That is all that is said about the Father. The core of the creed expands on what we believe about God the Father almighty by dwelling on what we know about Jesus Christ, his only begotten Son, our Lord. The core of the creed lies in what we affirm about Jesus Christ. After the creed has made clear our affirmation on the person and work of Jesus Christ, then the writers of the creed simply say, "I believe in the Holy Spirit." We will see in a moment that it is appropriate for us to spend such a succinct phrase of affirmation is appropriate, because it is not the responsibility of the Holy Spirit to call attention to himself.

Who is the Holy Spirit and what does he do? The Holy Spirit is the third person of the triune Godhead. The Bible tells us that there is only one God, but that this God exists in three persons: Father, Son, and Holy Spirit. The best efforts at explaining how we believe in one God, and yet this one God is three persons, would still leave us at a point where we would have to take a leap of faith to believe it; we do not fully understand it. The word *trinity* is never used in the Bible. Yet the Bible refers to the Father, to the Son, and to the Holy Spirit as three different persons, each possessing the same qualities. The word *trinity* is the word that the Christian church uses to refer to this God who is Father, Son, and Holy Spirit.

Let me suggest a chronological or experiential way that might help in understanding the doctrine of the Trinity and the work of the Holy Spirit. When we think of God the Father, we think of One who is before the Son, One who is more in the past, remote from us. He is the One who created the heavens and the earth. He is the invisible God, whom we know is there, yet long ago and far away. He is unreachable for us. But when we speak of the Son, we speak of One who came into this world two thousand years ago, but who has ascended into heaven and is above us. He is in the past and he is above us, and we are told that he is going to come again.

But when we speak of the Holy Spirit, we are speaking of God in the present tense. Jesus says, "If you love me, you will obey what I command. And I will ask the Father, and He will give you another Counselor to be with you forever—the Spirit of truth. The world cannot accept Him, because it neither sees Him nor knows Him.

But you know Him, for He lives with you and will be in you. I
will not leave you as orphans; I will come to you" (John 14:
15–18).

The Holy Spirit is not a neuter, a thing. The Holy Spirit is a
person. The Holy Spirit is referred to in the Scripture as having
knowledge, a will, a mind. He loves, grieves, speaks, prays for us,
teaches us, leads us. He is a person. He is God available to us now.

So what does he do? It is not within the scope of this chapter to
condense the hundreds of volumes that have been written on the
Holy Spirit. But a good way to begin to understand the Holy Spirit
is to start with the words of Jesus to his disciples during the week
immediately before the crucifixion: "It is for your good that I am
going away. Unless I go away, the Counselor will not come to you;
but if I go, I will send Him to you. . . . When He, the Spirit of
truth, comes, He will guide you into all truth. He will speak only
what He hears, and He will tell you what is yet to come. He will
bring glory to Me by taking from what is mine and making it
known to you" (John 16:7–14).

Imagine yourself as one of those original disciples, having lived
with Jesus for three years, watching him perform miracles, listening
to him teach, being close to him, and sensing that in him there is
something unique? Could you have believed it when he told you
that he was going to leave and yet that would be to your advantage?

How many times have you thought, If only I could have been
there with Jesus; if only I could have watched him heal the sick; if
only I could have heard Him teach; if only I could have talked to
him; if only I could have been an eyewitness to his miracles, it would
be so much easier to believe.

As difficult as it may be to understand, it is easier for us to believe
in Jesus today than it was for Jesus' contemporaries. The Holy Spirit
dwelling within the believer can do more for us today than the
living, physical presence of Jesus Christ could have done two thousand years ago.

Why is that true? Let me suggest a spiritual reason and a psychological reason. The spiritual reason is that the Holy Spirit helps us to
believe and understand the totality of Jesus' life and teaching. The

Holy Spirit is the inward Teacher who leads us into truth. The psychological reason is that if we could physically be with Jesus our perception of his life and ministry would be colored by all of the subtle prejudices evoked by physical appearance, cultural caste, and language accent. Because Jesus was fully human, had we been with him physically, we would have had to overcome our perception of him as only human. After the resurrection even the disciples still thought of Jesus in human political terms. "Lord, are you at this time going to restore the kingdom to Israel?" (Acts 1:6). Jesus' reply was to tell them to stay in Jerusalem until they had been baptized with the Holy Spirit (Acts 1:7–8).

When Jesus left the disciples, he removed himself from them physically and sent the Holy Spirit to dwell in each believer. The Holy Spirit would help the disciples recall all that Jesus taught. The Holy Spirit would be the one who would convict people of sin. The Holy Spirit would be the one to convince people of the truth. The Holy Spirit would be the believer's comforter and guide.

In John 16:14 Jesus said, "He will bring glory to me by taking from what is mine and making it known to you." One of my concerns about the charismatic or neo-pentecostal movement is that people in that movement call attention to the Holy Spirit and to their experience of the Spirit's power. Jesus said that the Holy Spirit would "bring glory to me," meaning Jesus. A friend of mine put it this way: "The Holy Spirit is the shy member of the Trinity." He does not call attention to himself. He calls attention to Jesus Christ, and where Jesus Christ is lifted up we know the Spirit is at work. Where the Holy Spirit becomes the focal point of attention, I am not sure who is at work. I say that as a word of warning, because we are told in Romans 12, 1 Corinthians 12, and Ephesians 4 that the Holy Spirit is the source of the gifts, the talents, and abilities that build the church. I believe that every one of those gifts that are listed in those chapters, plus other gifts of which those are only a symbol, are gifts that are applicable to the church today. But when those gifts occur, whether it is preaching, teaching, working miracles, or speaking in tongues, they are authentic only if they glorify Christ—not the Holy Spirit, and not the person who exercises the gift.

The Holy Spirit is not only the source of the gifts that Christ gives to his church, but the Holy Spirit is also the producer of fruit: the qualities of life that are evidence of the life of God.

In writing to the Christians in Galatia, Paul writes, "The fruit of the Spirit is love, joy, peace, patience, kindness, goodness, faithfulness, gentleness and self-control" (Gal. 5:22–23). He speaks of the fruit of the Spirit as the things that give evidence that God's life is present.

The Bible tells us that the Holy Spirit is given to everyone who believes in the Lord Jesus Christ. For the Spirit to be present in your life does not mean that he has control of your life. He may be resident but he may not be reigning. Paul says in his letter to the Christians in Ephesus, "Be filled with the Spirit" (Eph. 5:18). It is not enough for us to say, "I believe in the Holy Spirit." The question is, Are we open to the Spirit's control of our lives? Do we experience the fullness of life Jesus promised to those who know him? Are we using the gifts he has given us for the building up of the church? Is the fruit of the Spirit, those qualities of life that mark God's presence, evident in our lives?

The church in China grew tremendously under Communist domination of that country. When the last missionary was expelled from China in 1953, there were an estimated two to three million Christians in China. I have heard estimates that today there are between thirty million and fifty million Christians in China. The church has mushroomed under persecution. Why? The government would not allow the exercise of the gifts of the Spirit, such as preaching, teaching, and evangelism. Those things that generally mark the corporate life of the church, the government suppressed. But what could the government not suppress? It could not suppress the fruit of the Spirit! As a Christian exhibited love, joy, peace, patience, and kindness in the midst of persecution, he or she would be approached by other Chinese, who would ask, "How in the world can you have love and joy in times like these?" Then the Christian would share the Good News of the living presence of Christ, and so the Church grew.

It is when we as Christians are filled with the Spirit of God that the world will sit up and take notice. Others will ask, "How can I have that love and that joy and that peace?" They will come to know Christ through the witness of common believers in whom the Holy Spirit produces his fruit.

I believe in the Holy Spirit, who is God in the present tense. Is he present in your life today in all of his fullness?

Chapter 10

HOW BIG IS THE CHURCH?

"I Believe in . . . the Holy Catholic Church."

How important is the church in the life of a Christian?

Which church is the best church?

Does any church have the right to claim to be exclusively the true church?

Does the existence of hypocrites and bad people in a church mean that it is not a good church?

In the light of recent scandals about immorality and mishandling of funds in churches and religious organizations, such questions are very legitimate.

The Apostles' Creed refers to the church in a simple statement: "I believe in . . . the holy catholic church."

Did you know that when any congregation meets on a Sunday morning, there are really two different churches gathered in the sanctuary? One church is obvious. It is the visible church. It is called the visible church because it can be seen. The membership of the visible church is made up of those who profess faith in Jesus Christ, together with their children. This visible church generally is characterized by the reading of Scripture, singing, preaching, teaching, organization, and programs.

The other church gathered in the sanctuary is the invisible church. It is called invisible because its true membership is not defined by any written records that are kept by human beings, but only by the angels in the Lamb's Book of Life. The Westminster Confession of Faith puts it this way: "The invisible Church consists of the whole number of the elect that have been, are, or shall be gathered into one under Christ, the head, and is His bride, His body; the fullness of Him Who fills all in all."

Let's put it another way. Not everyone who is a member of the visible church, and has his or her name on the church roll, is necessarily a member of the true church, the real body of Christ. Not everybody who professes to be a Christian really is.

To say this is not in any way passing judgment upon anyone. God is the One who knows our hearts; and God is the One who ultimately determines whether our faith is genuine or false, whether our membership in the visible church really is a membership in the invisible church. But it is a basic and important fact of the biblical teaching about the followers of Jesus Christ that there are some people who are "tag-alongs," who really are not a genuine part of the body of Christ. Jesus told his disciples the parable about a farmer who sowed good seed in the field but at night an enemy sowed tares, a plant that in its early stages looks like wheat. When the wheat and tares began to reach maturity, it became obvious to the servants that the purity of the crop had been compromised. They wanted to go into the field and pull up the tares. The farmer said, "No, lest in pulling up the tares you hurt the wheat. Wait, and at the harvest time the two will be separated" (Matt. 13:24–30). Jesus was saying that the Kingdom of God on Earth will never be free from impurities.

The distinction between the visible and the invisible church is important for two reasons. It is important not to expect of the visible church a perfection that the Bible tells us is impossible. Even if everyone in the visible church was truly a member of the invisible church, the church still would not be perfect, because Christians are not perfect—they are just on the way. And the truth is that there always have been and always will be hypocrites in the church.

The other reason it is important to keep this distinction in mind is to avoid defining the church with boundaries that are too small. The true church, whose membership is known only to our Lord, must never be equated with only one denomination or one particular congregation.

What are we affirming when we say that we believe "in. . . . the holy catholic church?" From time to time I get a letter from someone who has heard me preach in my church or on television, asking why we, in a Presbyterian church, believe in the Catholic church.

Note that the word *catholic* is not capitalized. The word means "universal," and when we affirm faith in the church we are affirming the universal nature of the Body of Christ, as opposed to any particular denomination or congregation.

Believing in the Church has never been a critical issue. From the time of the Old Testament "church in the wilderness" under the leadership of Moses, until this day, believers recognize and generally approve "the church." Even people who are not members say, "Sure, I believe in the church. People want to get together, worship, have fellowship, do their own thing. That is fine."

The critical issue throughout the history of the church has been, Just how big is the church? How inclusive is it? From the earliest days of the Christian era the teaching of our Lord and his disciples has been that the church is holy and the church is catholic. That is what we affirm in the phrase of the Apostles' Creed concerning the church: "I believe in . . . the holy catholic church." Except for the phrase, "He descended into hell," which is included in some versions of the Apostles' Creed, this affirmation causes more controversy among Protestants than any other part of the creed.

Obviously these people do not understand what the word means. As we consider what we mean when we say, "I believe in . . . the holy catholic church," let us first define what we mean when we speak about the church. The word *church* comes from the Greek word *ekklesia,* which is a combination of two Greek words: *ek,* meaning "out of," and *kaleo,* meaning "called." The church of Jesus Christ is that body of people who have responded to the message of the gospel and who, in distinction from the rest of the world, are identified as belonging to Jesus Christ. They are called by God, have responded to him, and now are a part of that group of people known as the body of Christ.

The Israelites in the Old Testament were called a church. Stephen, the first martyr, in his defense before the Sanhedrin just before they stoned him, referred to Moses being with the "ekklesia in the wilderness" (Acts 7:38). The King James Version translates the Greek word as *church* whereas the New International Version uses the word *assembly*. The Old Testament people of God were a church in that they were called out by God to belong to him. But the Old Testament church was a church that was characterized by national boundaries. It was local to a particular part of the world, and to become a part of that church you either had to be born into it, or you had to profess faith in the one true God and submit yourself to the rituals and regulations of the Jewish faith. The Old Testament church always had to fight against being ingrown. One of the major dangers, and one of the major sins for which the prophets castigated the people, was that the people of God seemed to think they were chosen for privilege rather than responsibility. They viewed themselves as that enclave of God to which the rest of the people of the world should come if they wanted to be blessed.

The prophet Jonah had to struggle against that deep sense of national loyalty. He was convinced that God was concerned only for the Jews and not for other people. Furthermore, his desires were influenced by self-interest. The very city to which he was called to go and preach, Nineveh, was the capital of Assyria, a nation that posed a great military threat to Israel. He would have loved to have seen Nineveh destroyed. Yet God said—and here I am paraphrasing Jonah 1—"Go and preach, because if they do not repent, I will destroy them." Jonah naturally was torn. His deep sense of loyalty to his own country led him to run away from the commission that God had given him, because he would just as soon have seen the capital city of Assyria destroyed by God's judgment. That sense of narrowness, of being chosen for privilege, was one of the sins of the Old Testament congregation.

That was also one of the problems with the New Testament church. The New Testament Christians felt blessed by God in a special way, and they wanted to enjoy the fellowship there in Jerusalem. It was Jesus who said to them, "Go into all the world and preach the Good News to all creation" (Mark 16:15). He gave them a commission to go, but they preferred to stay and let the world come to them.

Jesus founded the church on a very specific truth. On one occasion he asked the disciples, "Who do people say that I am?"

Peter said, "You are the Christ, the Son of the living God."

Jesus turned to Peter and said, "Peter, upon this rock [the truth of your confession], I will build My Church" (Matt. 16:13–20).

The confession of Jesus Christ as Savior and Lord, as the Son of God, is the foundation of the church. People who profess faith in him are the building blocks. In that sense the Church is narrow. It has a very specific foundation. The Church is not inclusive of every idea. It is inclusive only of the truth that is built on Christ.

But given that foundation of the confession of Jesus as Savior and Lord, the Apostle Paul could write to the Christians in Galatia, "You are all sons of God through faith in Christ Jesus, for all of you who were baptized into Christ have clothed yourselves with Christ. There is neither Jew nor Greek, slave nor free, male nor female, for you are all one in Christ Jesus. If you belong to Christ, then you are Abraham's seed, and heirs according to the promise" (Gal. 3:26–29). So the early church declared that in the church there are no nationalistic barriers, there are no cultural barriers, there are no class barriers, there are no gender barriers that separate us from one another or separate us from God. That does not, of course, mean that the differences are not there. But the affirmation of the New Testament is clear. None of those differences has any value in our fellowship, nor in our belonging to God, nor in our access to his gracious promises. So the church is catholic, that is, universal.

The church is made up of people who profess faith in Christ and who then belong to a body that is called catholic and that is called holy.

The word *holy* has a saccharine, overly pious connotation in our day; we may think of a holy person as one who has little contact with the world. How unfortunate! The word *holy* is an electric word. As used by the writers of the Apostles' Creed, it is a word that means "belonging to God." It is characterized by godly qualities. The concept of holiness is often equated with a list of things that we are to avoid; we congratulate ourselves on our perfection when we have kept those rules.

That is not what God calls holy. To be holy means to be attracted to God and to have his qualities reflected in us. To be holy is to value what God values. To be holy is to be valued by God and set apart for him.

Furthermore, we are called upon to love one another as God has loved us, with the initiative and the power and the grace and the self-sacrifice that God has given to us in Jesus Christ; that is to be the mark of the kind of love we have within the church. It is a much easier to draw up a list of things that we must not do, isn't it? It is hard to love one another as God has loved us. But holiness means belonging to God, and to be characterized by his life and his qualities.

Then the word 'catholic' means 'universal.' That means that the Church is not limited by racial, ethnic, gender, cultural, economic barriers. It does not have those limits. It crosses all of those boundaries.

Notice I have said nothing about any particular denomination or congregation. A biblical theology of the church understands that the church is bigger than the sum total of all churches in a denomination or country. Wherever the true church is found you will find people who profess faith in Jesus Christ, worship the triune God, celebrate the sacraments, and are governed by God's Word.

A woman was talking to her Presbyterian minister, taking him to task for injecting something into a worship service which, she said, was "not Presbyterian."

"Well," the minister replied, "you don't mean to say that you believe that the only way you can get to heaven is by being a Presbyterian, do you?"

She thought a minute and said, "No, not really. But no genteel person would think of going any other way."

Of course, we know there are people who may feel that sort of deep loyalty to a particular church or to their particular denomination. At the Presbyterian Congress on Renewal held in Dallas in 1985, Bruce Larson opened the first meeting by saying, "We are here at last. It is a little bit like heaven. We are surprised at some of the people we see, and some of the people we don't see." There are some folks who are going to be surprised, I think, when they get to heaven, at who is there and who is not. The point is that the church is bigger than our narrow, sectarian boundaries. It is no broader than the foundation that was laid, which is Christ Jesus. It is no more inclusive than that. But, my friends, let us remember it is as inclusive as that.

John Calvin said that the marks of the true Church are the Word of God truly preached, the sacraments of Jesus Christ rightly administered, and the life of godliness purely lived, which involves the discipline of the church. Wherever the church exists, there we find the Word of God preached, and the sacraments of Jesus Christ administered; and godly living comes as a result of those. The Westminster Confession of Faith in its chapter on the church gives some worthwhile restrictions. It says that the invisible church is more or less present in the visible church as we see the Word of God truly preached, the sacraments administered, and a life of godliness. It goes on to say that some churches have so departed from the Word of God, and from godly living, and from the right administration of the sacraments, as to be no churches at all.

What are the marks of the church? What are the facets of the church's life? When we read the New Testament we find that the life of the church is characterized by five things: the people who belong to the Church are people who worship, learn, gather in fellowship, witness, and serve.

And what about those organizations that we call the parachurch because they operate alongside of the church, but not under the auspices of the church? What about organizations such as Young Life, Campus Crusade, Youth for Christ, Inter-Varsity Christian Fellowship, and similar organizations?''

I believe these organizations are a parallel—a largely unrecognized parallel—of the Roman Catholic orders. The Protestant Reformation in the sixteenth century was a movement attempting to reform and to purify the church. When the established church opposed this reformation, the reformers did not leave the church; instead, they mostly were excommunicated. Only then did they form new institutions. They cleared out some of the things they perceived as being impurities in the church, but there were some pure things in the church that they did not carry over. One was the concept of orders. In the Roman Catholic church, if a group of people feels called to some special task, it can apply for permission to be organized into an order. That order is then recognized as being a part of the church with a specific job. If a group of people wants to form an order to reach teenagers for Christ, then the church should recognize them, bless them, and let them go about their work.

The Protestant church has no way of recognizing that. And it has become so institutionalized that unless the institutional leaders give their blessing, and they seldom do, these things just go on beside the church. That is where we get the idea of the parachurch. These groups operate outside the institutional church. Sometimes they are a crutch for the institutional church. How much healthier it would be if these organizations were recognized as a Protestant version of orders! And how much better it would be if the church acknowledged the specialized ministry of each group and allowed them to work together, supporting one another in their ministries! We need to understand the church as that group of people who profess faith in Jesus Christ; who seek to follow him; and who gather together to hear his word preached, to observe the sacraments, and to discipline themselves to godly living.

The issue is not whether we believe in the church, for we all do. The spiritual issue is how big do we see the church? My friends, I am convinced that when we get to heaven we are going to find that the church is a whole lot bigger than any of us had ever realized. Gathered together in heaven as the redeemed body of Christ, we are going to rejoice in how big the church in which we believe really is, and together we will praise our Lord, who is the head of the church.

Chapter 11

THE TIE THAT BINDS

"I Believe in . . . the Communion of Saints."

In the fall of 1966 it was my privilege to attend the World Congress on Evangelism in West Berlin, Germany. This gathering of Christians from all over the world highlighted the message of the gospel of God's love for all people, and his provision of salvation in Jesus Christ, as well as the methods by which the Good News could be shared with the world.

But the posterior can tolerate only so much of a good thing, and after eight days of sitting and listening and being inspired and informed, I had an idea. I had recently read a biography of Martin Luther, that godly yet earthy reformer of the sixteenth century, who had started the Reformation in Wittenberg, Germany, by nailing ninety-five propositions for debate with church authorities on the door of the castle church in Wittenberg. After inquiry, I found Wittenberg was only a couple of hours away. But it was in East Germany. I asked a friend who had helped in preparing for the congress if a bus could be chartered, and, if so, if it would be possible to get into East Germany and drive to Wittenberg. He said yes to the chartering, and that he would find out about the trip to Wittenberg. When he told me later that it could be done, I went to some other friends and acquaintances in attendance, and shared with them the idea. The response was enthusiastic. It did not take very long to get together twenty-seven persons for a trip the next day. Early in the process of planning for that trip someone said to me, "Be sure to ask Dr. Oswald Hoffman to go." I did not know Dr. Hoffman, and so I said, "Why Dr. Hoffman?" "Because," this friend replied, "he knows more about Martin Luther than anyone else here at this congress." So I proceeded to look up Dr. Hoffman.

Dr. Hoffman is (as of this writing) the minister for the "Lutheran Hour," and one of the great preachers of this generation. He was also the adviser in the production of the film *Martin Luther*. He speaks German fluently. When I asked him if he would be interested in accompanying us on the trip, much to my delight, he jumped at the chance. Thus began an exciting excursion and a friendship that has continued to this day.

The next morning we boarded the bus and entered East Germany by going through Checkpoint Charlie. It was a dreary October day, and Wittenberg turned out to be a small, drab, and dreary town. We were greeted by a government guide, who welcomed us politely to Wittenberg and proceeded to give us the approved lecture. She then told the bus driver where to take us and we started on the tour.

I had placed Dr. Hoffman in the front seat of the bus so he could better communicate with us. Very early in our tour he interjected something about the history of Martin Luther, and it was not long before the guide, to whom he spoke in German, realized that he knew more about Martin Luther than she did. She was gracious enough to let him take over more and more of the tour. Dr. Hoffman talked and we looked. We went through the seminary where Martin Luther had taught and saw the apartment where he had lived. We learned something about the city's culture and history and ended up at the castle church.

From time to time, I would glance at the guide. Gradually I saw the muscles of her face relax. I saw a sparkle come into her eyes as she listened to Dr. Hoffman and as she observed the way we responded to what he was saying and what we were seeing. I could see the taut muscles of her shoulders gradually relax as she began to enjoy the trip.

When we gathered in the castle church, a large Gothic cathedral, the twenty-seven of us sang a cappella Luther's great hymn "A Mighty Fortress Is Our God." The walls echoed with the sound of that hymn. Here again I watched as she listened to us, and I could see smile lines appear at the corners of her eyes. She knew who we were and what was happening.

Shortly after that we boarded our bus for the return trip to West Berlin. She also got on the bus, but before the driver, and looking around carefully to see that none of her countrypeople was within earshot, she said, "Pray for us and God bless you."

The communion of the saints took place that day. Not in what she said, but in what took place deep in her heart and our hearts, before she spoke those words. She was aware in her own heart and soul, and the awareness gradually dawned on us as well, that even though we lived miles apart and were separated by geography and political ideology, here with her on that bus were brothers in Christ—for we were all men—and we saw in her a sister in Christ. We knew it. We sensed it. When she said, "Pray for us and God bless you," she was merely verbalizing a truth and giving outward expression to a reality that already existed.

In December of 1989 my wife and I spent five days in East Germany accompanied by Dr. and Mrs. Reinhold Kerstan, who served as driver and interpreter. We interviewed pastors, Christian laypersons, and in Erfurt I preached in a Baptist church. The communion of saints could be sensed everywhere we turned. Despite the barriers of language, nationality, political inclination, and sectarian difference, it was exciting to sense the bond of unity that came from our common faith in Jesus Christ.

Following the creedal statement "I believe in . . . the holy catholic church," comes this affirmation: "I believe in . . . the communion of saints." What does that mean?

The word *communion* means "fellowship plus." It is more than the good time that people have when kindred spirits get together. It is rather the comradeship of those who know and enjoy the knowledge that they share the same heritage, the same values, and the same destiny. It is a deep sense of meshing together at the level of the soul. When we say we believe in the communion of the saints, we are saying that in a church that is universal (catholic), and that belongs to God (holy), we are knit together in a common bond of love and devotion to the same Lord, and therefore knit together in a commitment to each other.

The phrase "the communion of saints" was one of the last phrases added to the Apostles' Creed. It first appeared in the fifth century A.D., in the writings of Nicetas. The words he used were the Latin words, *communio sanctorum*.

The meaning of the phrase "communion of the saints" is complicated but also enriched by the dual meaning of that Latin phrase. Those words can mean either "the fellowship of holy persons" (that is, those persons who are a part of the holy catholic church), or the phrase can mean, "participation in holy things." If the meaning is the latter, the reference is to the participation of believers in the sacraments of the church.

Given the historical setting of the day, I rather think that phrase was added to emphasize the importance of the sacraments. With the passage of time, we have come to think of it more as the fellowship of kindred hearts.

But we do not have to make a choice between those two emphases. I think it means both. Every time we gather together around the Lord's table for Communion, we gather for communion with our living Lord and for communion with one another in Christ. There is participation in holy things, but there is also a fellowship of kindred spirits.

What is happening when we take Holy Communion? What is the nature of the communion we have with Jesus Christ?

There are many different ways in which Communion is served, but the two elements that are common to all Christian observances of the sacrament are bread and wine (or grape juice). At the last supper Jesus had with his disciples, he instituted this sacrament by taking bread, breaking it, and giving it to them, saying, "This is my body which is broken for you." Then he took a cup of wine, passed it to the disciples, and said, "This is the new covenant in my blood" (Matt. 26:26–29).

Most protestants interpret Jesus' words about the bread being his body and the cup being the new covenant in his blood as describing a symbolic relationship between the elements and what he did by physically dying. We do not believe that the bread literally becomes the body of Christ, nor that the wine literally becomes the blood of Christ.

But the majority of Protestants also believe that Communion is much more than just a memorial supper, a perpetuation of the event that took place when Jesus had that last supper with his disciples.

When we come to Communion we believe that something mysterious and yet very real is taking place. When we eat the bread, we are participating in some mysterious way, by faith, with our living Lord and in the benefits that he purchased for us by his broken body. When we drink from the cup, we are participating in fellowship with our living Lord and what he purchased for us by shedding his blood on the cross. There is a mysterious correlation between what we do physically and what happens spiritually.

When Paul wrote to the Christians in Corinth, he lovingly and pastorally chastised them for their misuse of the sacrament. He said, "When you come to Communion, you are coming in such an unworthy way that you actually are guilty of profaning the body and the blood of Christ." Because of petty divisions and lack of repentance, they were coming to the table in a haughty spirit and with much animosity. Therefore, "Because you are partaking unworthily, some of you are sick, and some of you have actually died" (1 Cor. 11:17–32). There is such a close connection between Communion —the eating of the bread and the drinking of the cup—and what goes on in our hearts and lives, that either something very real of the grace of God is imparted, or the judgment of God falls.

So when we say that we believe in the communion of saints, we are saying that we believe that the possibility of communion with our Lord through the sacrament of Communion is so real that is has to be taken seriously. It must be taken carefully and it must be done with repentance, in humility and genuine faith. It is real.

But when we come to that table we come also as a Christian family. When we do that we are sharing with one another in a common commitment to Christ, whose body and blood are symbolized by the bread and wine. We say our faith is in him and what he has done for us. That makes us a family. As our Lord has been patient with us, we are to be patient with one another. As we have been forgiven by God, we are to forgive one another. As we have been loved by God, we are to love one another. As we have been supported and encouraged by God's Word, we are to support and encourage one another. The communion of the saints means that the relationship we have with Jesus Christ through faith is demonstrated through the elements of the Communion service and is lived out in the family sharing that faith.

But what does the word *saint* mean? We tend to think of a saint as somebody who is now dead, and who, while alive, lived an extraordinarily good life. Because of that extraordinary goodness, he or she is recognized by the church.

But that is not the way the New Testament uses the word *saint*. In fact, interestingly enough, there are sixty-two references to saints in the New Testament where the word is found in the plural. There is only one reference in the New Testament to *saint* in the singular. The word *saints* in the New Testament is the equivalent of believers. And saints are referred to not as extraordinarily good people, but as a part of those who are the saved ones, thus made holy by the blood of Christ. (See my discussion of the word *holy* in chapter 10.) "Saints" are the believers and the believers are "saints."

Is this communion of the saints something that we must work at, or is it something that already exists? Like the unity of the body of Christ, there is a sense in which it is true as a reality, and yet it needs practical expression, or demonstration. The communion of saints is something that does exist, and yet it can be breached, it can be damaged, it can be broken.

I experienced the communion of saints in Wittenburg in 1966, and throughout East Germany in 1989. I also experienced it on a trip to China. Several years ago I led a tour group to China, and on Sunday morning we asked to go to worship services. When we entered the church we discovered that it was Communion Sunday, and, even though none of us understood a word that was said, we knew what was going on. We sensed a oneness in Christ with that family of faith. We were one in Christ, and the communion that we shared in the sacrament carried over into a friendliness and openheartedness of fellowship after the service that defied all human explanation. The communion of saints is a reality.

But when we live and work with people on a regular basis, we discover that, as in marriage, it takes work to keep the relationship open, honest, and supportive. Without conscious effort, it is easy to breach that fellowship.

In I John 1:1–7, John, writing to some early Christians, says, "There is something which we have seen and handled and experienced. It is the life of God in human flesh. We share this with you, and that is the foundation of our fellowship. It is our commitment to Jesus Christ." It does not make any difference whether you go by the name of Presbyterian or Baptist or Methodist or Episcopalian or Lutheran or Roman Catholic. Those who are committed to Christ and who know him can experience this kind of communion that crosses the human boundaries that separate us. In our Lord's church there is no boundary that keeps us from God, and none that should keep us from one another. At the same time we recognize that this fellowship, this communion (koinonia is the Greek word), this close partnership in the gospel, is based first of all upon our common allegiance to the One who is the life of God in human flesh.

John goes on to say that the way we live affects that communion, particularly if we claim to be a part of the body of Christ and if we claim to be in the light, and yet we walk in darkness. John uses a very sharp word: he says that we are liars, because those in whom the light dwells walk in light.

What does it mean to walk in the light? It means consciously to walk in full disclosure. It means to live in such a way that we are not embarrassed for God to know what is going on. Of course he knows. We cannot hide anything from him, but we sometimes try to live as though God does not know. To walk in the light is simply to walk in the realization that we are exposed to him, and that we do not have to fear who finds out how we are living. That means that our conduct passes the scrutiny of God's goodness. If we do not walk that way, then the fellowship, the communion, is breached. When we walk in the light as he is in the light, we have fellowship, we have communion one with another. And he says that the blood of Jesus, his Son, cleanses us from all sin. We know forgiveness as we walk in the light.

There is a tie that binds us together with all believers of all ages. It is the tie of our common commitment to Jesus Christ. His life flows through us, and we are committed to walk according to the light God has given us in Jesus Christ and in his Word. Yes, we believe in the holy catholic, that is, universal, church, which belongs to God. In that church is a group of people called saints. They are saints not because they are perfect, but because they have communion with him; and having communion with him, they have communion with one another.

Yes, "I believe in . . . the communion of saints."

Chapter 12

THE GLORIOUS FREEDOM OF GRACE

"I Believe in . . . the Forgiveness of Sins."

Imagine yourself a criminal on death row. A well-intentioned historian comes into your cell and gives you a lecture on the great heritage of our nation; but inwardly you say to yourself, So what? Can you get me out of jail? Then a long-time friend of the president of the United States comes to tell you what a fine man he is and how much power he has in the world; and you cut him short by asking, "Will he get me off death row?" Someone else comes and tells you about a wonderful group of people who meet on a regular basis to give support to one another, encourage one another, and what a help they could be to you. You finally shout at her, "I don't give a rip about those folks unless they can get this noose from around my neck!"

Martin Luther, before he entered the priesthood and before he became the great reformer of the sixteenth century, was a man with a spiritual and emotional noose around his neck. He was haunted day and night by the guilt he felt and by the impending sense of divine doom that comes from the knowledge, even without the Bible spelling it out, that "the wages of sin is death."

It was not until several years after he entered the priesthood that Luther discovered the glorious freedom from guilt that comes from the grace of God in Jesus Christ. It is not surprising that Luther said that the phrase, "I believe in . . . the forgiveness of sins" was the most important article in the Apostles' Creed. Said Luther: "If that is not true, what does it matter whether God is almighty or that

Jesus Christ was born and died and rose again? It is because these things have a bearing upon my forgiveness that they are important to me." So if the previous articles of the creed were not true, there would be no possibility of forgiveness. And if the truth of the previous articles did not make possible our forgiveness, what good would that truth be?

There is no article of the Apostles' Creed that has greater practical importance for each of us than this affirmation: "I believe in . . . the forgiveness of sins."

Let us explore the meaning of this article of the creed by discussing four questions:

What is sin?
What does it mean to be forgiven?
How is forgiveness possible?
How is forgiveness received?

What is sin? The most concise definition ever penned is the Westminster Shorter Catechism answer to this very question. It states, "Sin is any want of conformity to or transgression of the law of God." On the one hand, sin is failure to live up to God's expectations; and on the other hand, sin is acting contrary to what God says we are to do. Often we focus our attention on the negative things— doing the things we have been told not to do—and we forget that sin is also a failure to do the things that God positively says we are to do. It is easy to say that sin is committing adultery or murder or theft or bowing down in front of idols. We are not quite so ready to admit that sin is failing to love God with all our hearts, souls, minds, and strength, or failing to love our neighbors as ourselves. But sin is *doing* what God says we should *not* do and *not doing* what God says we should do.

Still, this definition focuses our attention on *doing* or *not doing* what the law of God requires.

But is sin merely a matter of what you do or don't do? Or is there is a deeper dimension to sin that grows out of your spiritual character? Are you a sinner because you sin? Or do you sin because you are a sinner?

The Apostle Paul struggled with this in his own experience and wrote about it in Romans, chapter 7. Paul discovered that sin is the product of a spiritually defective person. He said, and I paraphrase, "I have come to grips with the terrible reality that there is a part of me that knows what is right, but I can't do it. Then there is another part of me that pulls me to do things that are wrong." He found himself caught up in this terrible struggle. With the mind he understood the high call of God to be good. There is an objective goodness that he knew that he ought to live by, but he could not do it. Then there was the baser side of him, which reached out to those things that he knew he should not do, but he found that he was powerless to control that inner base self.

When we talk about forgiveness, it is important to realize that we need not only to be forgiven for the things we *do* that are wrong, but we need forgiveness for *not doing* the things that are right. *And,* we need forgiveness for being the kind of people who sin.

We can understand the drastic need for forgiveness only when we can understand the awesome holiness of God. If you were to take a can of spray paint to a long-abandoned shack in the middle of nowhere and spray graffitti on its walls, probably no one would take notice. There would be little or no punishment. But if you were to take that same can of spray paint and go to the marbled walls of the local city hall, you would get quite a different reaction. Public officials and public sentiment would be greatly offended. If you were caught at it, you would have to pay a fine for marring public property, and probably would have to pay the expense for getting the offending paint removed. If you were to take that same can of spray paint to the local art museum and spray a painting by one of the great masters, you would not only get your name in the paper but you probably would be thrown in jail and assessed a hefty fine. Why? It's the same can of spray paint. Why the different reactions? The difference is in the object that is marred and the one (or ones) offended by the act.

If I were to get angry or frustrated and take out my feelings by kicking a tree, I might sprain my toe or break my ankle. But if I were to express those same emotions by kicking a trained attack dog, I would get a completely different reaction. The action would be the same and the motivation would be the same, but the object would be different.

If we understand sin to be only a violation of human community standards, we have a totally different idea of forgiveness than when we understand that sin is committed against a holy, righteous, and perfect God. The reason why sin is so serious is because it is a violation of the holiness and righteousness and purity of God himself.

Do you remember the biblical account, in 2 Samuel 11, of David and Bathsheba? From the roof of his palace David looked down on the neighboring roofs one evening and saw a beautiful woman taking a bath. (This was the Middle East, where homes were constructed with flat roofs, and such activity was not unusual.) David lusted after her, called her to the palace, and committed adultery with her. When he found out that she was pregnant, he sent for her husband, Uriah, who was fighting in a battle on the front lines. David's hope was that Uriah and Bathsheba would sleep together, and that the paternity of the child would thus be hidden. But Uriah, out of a sense of loyalty to his fellow soldiers, who were suffering the deprivations of war, refused to sleep with Bathsheba. David send him back to the front lines and ordered the commanding officer to withdraw the troops from him, leaving Uriah vulnerable.

Everything went just as David planned. Uriah was killed by the enemy. But David forgot one thing: it is possible to fool the public, but you can never fool God. God sent Nathan the prophet to confront David and show him what he had done. David was guilty of murder as well as adultery. When he realized how sinful he was and how heinous was his sin, he truly repented. Psalm 51 is the psalm he penned in remorse and repentance for his sin. In that psalm he said to God, "Against thee, thee only have I sinned." Wait a minute. How about Bathsheba? How about Uriah? Didn't David sin against them? He harmed them, yes. But the heinousness of his sin was the violation of God's righteousness and holiness.

We will never understand the drastic need for forgiveness until we understand that when we sin we have sinned not just against people;

we have violated not just the mores of our community. *We have violated the holiness of an absolutely holy God! We have offended the righteous standards of an absolutely righteous God! We have soiled the purity of God's absolute goodness with the impurity of our sin!*

What are the consequences of this outrage against God?

Because we have sinned against a God who is eternally righteous and holy, our punishment must be in keeping with the character of the One against whom we have sinned. In short, sin against an eternal God must receive an eternal punishment.

And just because we have forgotten some sin doesn't mean that God has. God is eternal. That means that he exists independent of our time frame. Our time frame places everything into past, present, and future. To God, everything is present. Sins we committed years ago and have forgotten about, we are still committing in God's eyes. They may be past to us, but they are present to God.

What does it mean to be forgiven? It means to have God, who is eternal and before whom our actions have eternal continuation, say "your sins are blotted out." That is one of the phrases used in the Bible about the forgiveness of sins. God says, "I will blot out your transgressions. I will erase your sins. I will remove your sins as far from Me as the east is from the west" (Ps. 103:12).

How far is that? That is an eternal distance. When you are headed west, you are always going west. When you are headed east, you are always going east, and "never the twain shall meet." When God says, he will blot out your transgressions, he is saying that he will erase them. It is like erasing a tape. The prophet Micah uses a different figure of speech when he affirms, "You will again have compassion on us; you will tread our sins underfoot and hurl all our iniquities into the depths of the sea (Micah 7:19). Forgiveness means that God no longer tries to collect what you owe him.

Why is forgiveness so important? What makes it so necessary?

Forgiveness of sins is important because the price of sin is so terrible. The Scripture says, "The wages of sin is death, but the gift of God is eternal life through Jesus Christ, our Lord" (Rom. 6:23).

What are the practical consequences of this forgiveness?

Imagine yourself deeply in debt to someone. What if you cannot pay that debt? When you go to your creditor and tell her you cannot pay the debt, she has the legal right to exact penalties, put you in bankruptcy, and somehow try to recover at least a portion of the money. Or your creditor can say, "I will forgive you the debt." What does it mean when she forgives you the debt? It means that she treats you as though you no longer owe her any money. She no longer tries to collect what you owe her.

When we are forgiven by God, he no longer tries to collect the debt we owe him. As Mrs. H. M. Hall in the gospel hymn "Jesus Paid It All" puts it,

> Jesus paid it all,
> all to Him I owe;
> Sin had left a crimson stain,
> He washed it white as snow.

The first practical result of forgiveness is the lifting of the burden of guilt and feeling clean before God, because he has made us clean.

The second practical result of forgiveness is in the way we treat others who have sinned against us.

As *forgiven people* we are to live as *forgiving people*. When we ask God to "forgive us our debts as we forgive our debtors," which we do every time we pray The Lord's Prayer, we are asking God to be as forgiving of our sins as we are forgiving of the sins committed against us. It means that if someone hurts you, and then asks you to forgive him, you cannot collect the debt he owes you.

I discovered the real meaning of this a number of years ago. I had been terribly hurt by an injustice someone had done to me. I confronted the individual and, after the confrontation, that person acknowledged that he had done wrong and he asked my forgiveness. I said, "I will forgive you." But some months later I told someone else about the way I had been hurt. I was still chafing under the injustice, and my reason for retelling the story was to get even, to "collect the debt" by diminishing that person's reputation. I had not forgotten and I had not forgiven. When I discovered this unflattering truth about myself, what could I do? It is obvious that I still haven't forgotten, for I am retelling this incident, except without using names. But I confessed my lack of forgiveness to the Lord, and with his help, I will never again try to collect the debt by hurting that person's reputation.

When we say, "I believe in . . . the forgiveness of sins," we are saying that we believe that God cancels the debt that we owe him and he no longer tries to collect payment. If "the wages of sin is death," that means that when sin is forgiven, God no longer exacts the death penalty.

How is forgiveness possible? If God is holy and righteous and just, how is it that God can blot out our sins and treat us as though we do not owe him anything anymore? The debt had to be paid, and there was only one way that that could be done. That, of course, is the glorious Good News of the gospel of Jesus Christ. When Christ died on that cross two thousand years ago, he died not as a martyr who was giving his life out of faithfulness to a good cause. Rather, he died there for you and for me. He took our place on the cross. He paid our death penalty.

Now the Father looks at the debt we owe him for our sin, and across that debt, written in the blood of Jesus Christ, appears the word *canceled*. Or better yet, the Divine Judge erases the bill. When we receive a bill that says "canceled" or "paid in full," we can still see what is written behind it. But not so with the debt we owe God. He blots it out. He remembers it no more. God forgets it. That is the glorious freedom that comes from the marvelous grace of God, who forgives us, not because we deserve it, but because of the death of his Son.

How is forgiveness received? If it is provided for us, what do we have to do to receive it and make it real in our lives?

The Scripture says that there are several clear, definite steps to receiving God's forgiveness.

The *first* step is to repent of sin. *To repent* comes from a Greek word that means a total change of heart about something. Repentance is saying, "I'm not only sorry for what I did that was wrong, or for failing to do what was right, but I am sorry also for being the kind of person who falls short of God's perfect plan. I am sorry that I am a sinner who commits sin, and I give God permission to make me over again from the inside out." That is what leads you to being born from above, or born again, becoming a new creation in Christ.

Repentance is best illustrated, I think, by the prodigal son (Luke 15:11–32). This son took his inheritance and went away from home and his father's control. After squandering all of his inheritance, he ended up feeding pigs and eating their diet. He finally came to himself and realized how ridiculous it was for him to live that kind of life. He could do better working for his father. He would go back to his father and ask him to hire him as a servant. He turned his back on the pig pen and headed home. That is repentance: it is being sorry and more than sorry. It means being sorry enough to turn your back on a life of willful disobedience to God.

The *second step* to forgiveness is confession.

Confession means to agree with God in his assessment of our actions and character. God simply asks that we agree with him that his evaluation of sin is really true, and apply that evaluation to ourselves. "If we confess our sins, He is faithful and just to forgive us our sins and to cleanse us from all unrighteousness" (1 John 1:9). He only asks that we agree with him.

This is why, in dealing with sin, we must never pretend that sin is not sin. If we pretend that sin is not sin, then there is no forgiveness for it. The most loveless thing we can do to people is to make them feel fine about their sins, as though they were something less than an awful affront to the glorious holiness of God.

Once we have repented of being the kind of people who sin, and then have confessed our sins by agreeing with his evaluation of our lives and our conduct, then the *third step* to being forgiven is the act of faith in accepting his gift of forgiveness. Forgiveness is God's gift. We cannot deserve it. If we could deserve it, then it would be the result of our earning it. But because Christ died for us "while we were still sinners" (Rom. 5:8), forgiveness is offered as a gift, and when we accept the gift, we become acceptable in God's sight. The Son gives us entrance into the Father's family.

Yes, I believe in the forgiveness of sins because God has made it possible through Jesus Christ, and because the holy and righteous

God cannot be approached unless he forgives us and deals with us as people whose sins are blotted out. "But with You there is forgiveness;" says the psalmist, "therefore You are feared" (Ps. 130:4).

How wonderful, how glorious, *is* this Good News! We do not have to live with the burden of guilt. We do not have to live under the threat of an eternal death penalty. We can accept the Father's forgiveness, and we can live in the joyous freedom of his grace. Because Jesus died for us, we "believe in . . . the forgiveness of sins."

Chapter 13

THIS OLD HOUSE

"I Believe in . . . the Resurrection of the Body."

Thirty-five years ago Stuart Hamblen wrote a song that Rosemary Clooney made popular. The song was entitled, "This Ole House." The event that inspired its writing, as best I recall, went something like this: Stuart Hamblen was hunting high up in the Sierras. Topping a ridge, he came upon an old house that seemed about ready to fall apart. Some windowpanes were broken, shutters hung at crooked angles, many of the shingles on the roof were missing, some of the boards that formed the porch were gone, and the door, as he said, "looked like it had been in a wrestling match with a storm." Yet there were signs that somebody had recently lived there, so he called out as he approached the house. There was no answer. But as he drew near, an old hound dog came out of the house, stretched itself wearily, and lay down on the porch. Hamblen knew that he was not on deserted property, for no dog will stay long at a place if its master or mistress isn't there. He looked in the front room but it was vacant. Then he looked in the back room. There on a couch was the body of an old man. Some snow lay on his chest, blown in through a broken windowpane. Old curtains, signs of a woman's touch, hung at the windows. Looking around further, Hamblen saw a toy wagon with three wheels, indicating that at one time a child had called this place home.

The pathos of that scene impressed itself on his songwriter's mind, and, taking an old paper bag from his pocket, he wrote the song that became an international hit. The words, put to a Country Western tune, are as follows:

This ole house once knew my children,
This ole house once knew my wife,
This ole house was home and comfort
As we fought the storms of life;
This ole house once rang with laughter;
This ole house heard many a shout;
Now she trembles in the darkness when the light'nin'
    walks about.

This ole house is agettin' shaky,
This ole house is agettin' old,
This ole house lets in the rain,
This ole house lets in the cold,
On my knees I'm gettin' chilly,
But I feel no fear or pain,
'Cause I see an angel peeking through
    a broken windowpane.

This ole house is afraid of thunder,
This ole house is afraid of storms,
This ole house just groans and trembles,
When the night wind flings its arms,
This ole house is gettin' feeble,
This ole house is needin' paint.
Just like me, it's tuckered out,
    But I'm gettin' ready to meet the saints.

My old hound-dog lies a-sleepin',
He don't know I'm gonna' leave
Else he'd wake up by the fireplace
He'd just sit an' howl an' grieve;
But my huntin' days are over,
We ain't goin' huntin' anymore;
Gabriel done brought in my chariot
When the wind blew down the door!

Chorus: Ain't agonna need this house no longer,
          Ain't agonna need this house no more;
          Ain't got time to fix the shingles;

Ain't got time to fix the floor;
Ain't got time to oil the hinges nor
to mend the windowpane;
Ain't agonna need this house no longer,
I'm agettin' ready to meet the saints.*

Stuart Hamblen wrote that song to depict not only the disinte-
gration of a house made of brick and mortar, but also to symbolize
the deterioration of the human body with age. But to affirm that we
believe in the resurrection of the body might come as small conso-
lation to those people who, like this old man in his last days, have
reason to be unhappy with the bodies that they have. One woman
crippled with a bone disease that had left her stooped and deformed
said to me, "Preacher, if you're talking about the resurrection of this
body, forget it. It's not much to look forward to."

So when we affirm, "I believe in . . . the resurrection of the
body," what are we saying? What are we really affirming that in any
way is Good News? What does the Scripture teach us about the
body and life after death?

Christians were not the first to believe that there is life beyond this
existence. God created us human beings, with a sense that there is
something beyond this life.

Solomon wrote, "You have set eternity in the hearts of men"
(Eccles. 3:11). Indeed God has. It is apparently a fact of worldwide
experience that people think about life after death; and in thinking
about it, there is a universal sense of needing to be prepared for it.
Socrates and Plato believed in the immortality of the soul, but they
did not believe in the resurrection of the body. Various religions and
philosophies have affirmed the reality of continued existence, but
none of them has identified this existence with the resurrection of
the body. Some religions see each mortal as having within him or
her a spark of the divine, which will live forever. Some teach that at
death the spark of divinity reunites with the divine eternal whole.

---

* From the book, The Birth of a Song, © 1989 Hamblen Family Trust. Song words
copyright 1954, Re. 1982 by Hamblen Music Co., P.O. Box 1937 Canyon Country,
CA 91351. International Copyright secured. All rights reserved. Used by Permission.

Just as a drop of water may have an independent identity at some point during its existence but is then reunited with the ocean, so the soul, at death, becomes a part of a total mass of unidentifiable divinity.

But that is not what the Bible teaches. The Bible teaches us that we are unique individuals. We are created spiritually in the image of God. God has put us in identifiable bodies, and in the course of this life we, through our bodies, express our obedience and our discipleship, or our disobedience and our rebellion. It is through these bodies that we give expression to this faith that we claim. The Christian faith teaches us that when death comes the body dies, but there will come a time when that body will be raised again.

In 1 Corinthians 15, Paul affirms the resurrection of Jesus Christ. This passage of Scripture is central and crucial to the Christian gospel. When we say that we believe in the resurrection of the body, we affirm first that we believe that Jesus' body was raised from the dead. His resurrection is the very foundation of the Christian faith. Without that resurrection there would be no Christian faith. Jesus' resurrection was verified because he was recognized. And the disciples knew that they were not looking at a ghost because they saw the nail and spear scars in his hands and feet and side, they touched him, and they saw him eat food.

Yet there was something different about this postresurrection body. It could function differently than it had before his death. His resurrected body had a new quality. It did not require food or sleep. It had the power to appear and disappear. It had the power to move about without the normal limitations of space and time. It had the power to pass through locked doors. Still, it was a body that could be seen and touched and was very real.

Therefore the initial reason for affirming that we "believe in . . . the resurrection of the body" is because we believe that Jesus' body was raised from the dead. The Apostle Paul, writing to the Christians in Philippi, said, "But our citizenship is in heaven. And we eagerly await a Savior from there, the Lord Jesus Christ, who, by the power that enables him to bring everything under his control, will transform our lowly bodies so that they will be like his glorious body (Phil. 3:20–21). In that phrase we are told that our resurrected bodies will be like the resurrected body of Jesus.

When we affirm the resurrection of the body, what do we mean? What will it be like? What are some of the characteristics of this resurrection body? In the latter part of 1 Corinthians 15 and also in Luke 24, some attributes of the resurrection body are named. Let me mention seven. You may think of more.

First, the resurrected body will not be the same body that is laid in the grave. In 1 Corinthians 15:35–41 we read,

But someone may ask, "How are the dead raised? With what kind of body will they come?" How foolish! What you sow does not come to life unless it dies. When you sow, you do not plant the body that will be, but just a seed, perhaps of wheat or of something else. But God gives it a body as he has determined, and to each kind of seed he gives its own body. All flesh is not the same: Men have one kind of flesh, animals have another, birds another and fish another. There are also heavenly bodies and there are earthly bodies; but the splendor of the heavenly bodies is one kind, and the splendor of the earthly bodies is another. The sun has one kind of splendor, the moon another and the stars another; and star differs from star in splendor.

The human body is suited ideally for our life in this world. What Paul says is that the resurrected body is going to be different to the extent that it must be suited ideally for heaven and eternity.

Second, the resurrected body is not a body of flesh and blood. In 1 Corinthians 15:50–51 we read; "I declare to you, brothers, that flesh and blood cannot inherit the kingdom of God, nor does the perishable inherit the imperishable. Listen, I tell you a mystery: We will not all sleep, but we will all be changed."

When Paul speaks here of flesh and blood, he is talking about a body that is produced by and operates by normal biological processes. Blood is essential to the functioning of the body. This is why some people after a traumatic accident or surgery have to have blood transfusions. Without blood there is no life. The Scripture says that "the life of a creature is in the blood" (Lev. 17:11).

This is the reason that God required the Jews of the time of the Old Testament, when offering the sacrifice of atonement, to offer an animal sacrifice, which required shedding the blood of the animal. This is why Jesus died on a cross and shed his blood. He gave his life for us. Without the blood there is no life.

Paul says that the resurrected body is not a body of flesh and blood because the resurrected body no longer needs, and, indeed, no longer can thrive on, the same life source as the human body does in this world. It needs a different life source and it has it.

Also, the resurrected body will not be pure spirit, but will also have flesh and bones. Now that sounds like a contradiction, but it is not. Note that it is not flesh and blood, but it does have flesh and bones. It has structure; it has form. The sustaining life element in the human body, however, is missing, because the spiritual body does not need the blood. Speaking to his disciples in Luke 24:39, who are astonished at seeing him, thinking that they are seeing a ghost, Jesus says, "Look at my hands and my feet. It is I myself! Touch me and see; a ghost does not have flesh and bones, as you see I have." Jesus Christ was not a ghost. He had a physical body, and yet it was different. It is a mystery that we cannot fully explain. But we do believe in the power of God, who can bring back to life our physical bodies, and yet make them substantially different, so that they are suited for the life ahead. And we dare to believe this because he did it for Jesus' body.

Further, the Scripture teaches us that the resurrected body will not be subject to decay or corruption. 1 Corinthians 15:42 says, "So will it be with the resurrection of the dead. The body that is sown is perishable, it is raised imperishable." We are all very much aware of the perishableness of human life. We have buried loved ones. We have seen people get sick. We have been ill. We have been in accidents. One of the great motivating powers of life is the drive for self-preservation. We are all too aware of the fragility, the vulnerability, of the human body. But God has assured us that the resurrection body will not be subject to decay or corruption.

Yet another characteristic of this resurrection body is that it will be a glorious body. We read in 1 Corinthians 15:43 that the physical body "is sown in dishonor, it is raised in glory." The word *dishonor* is hardly a word that most would use as they lay a loved one in the grave. We do not think of the body as a dishonorable thing until we understand what the Greek word for *dishonor* means. The Greek word *atimia* means that the body is subject to the disgrace of passions and weakness. That, after all, is why we die. We are subject to the disgrace of passions and the disgrace of weakness: the hatred of people who kill one another; the drunkenness of a person who drives his car headon into innocent people; or the ravages of cancer, or heart ailments, or other diseases; and if nothing else gets us, the final deterioration of the aging process. These are the things that happen to the body that cause us to lay loved ones in the ground, and that will someday bring us to the same end.

The Scripture says that the body of the believer is placed in the ground (sown) because it is subject to passions and weakness. But it will be raised "in glory." The word *glory* (*doxa*) comes from the same word where we get the word *doxology*. It will be raised in glory, magnificence, splendor. What we sow, Paul says, is just an infinitesimal sample of what is to be. We take a grain of wheat and put it in the ground. The principle of life within it brings it forth in a magnificent little stem that has on it many multiplications of itself. If we can accept the magnificent wonder of the expansive multiplication of seeds we plant in this earth, then we can get some inkling of the magnificence of what is going to come forth from the grave when our bodies, which are sown in dishonor, are raised in glory.

Still further, the resurrected body will be a body full of power. The last half of 1 Corinthians 15:43 states, "it is sown in weakness, it is raised in power."

A friend said to me the other day, "My spirit makes commitments that my body can't keep." After the resurrection the body will be able to accomplish everything that the spirit wishes. Even now the spirit dreams things that it cannot begin to accomplish. We have ideas of good that we ought to achieve, but we cannot accomplish it because of the weakness of the flesh. But after the resurrection weariness and powerlessness will be gone; the bodies that we have after the resurrection will be bodies that can accomplish everything that God intends for us to accomplish.

Finally, the resurrected body will be ideally suited for heaven. In

1 Corinthians 15:47–49, Paul contrasts two classes of persons. There is the man of the earth, called Adam, and there is the Man from heaven, Jesus Christ. We who live on this earth are children of Adam, people of dust. But when we are raised again, our living Lord will give us bodies like his. So to say that we believe in the resurrection of the body is to affirm that we believe that we will rise from the dead just as Jesus did. We believe that the individuality of personhood is not lost, but lives on. We will be identifiable. We will know our loved ones in heaven. We will be recognized. Yet all of the imperfections, all of the flaws, all of the failures of our human bodies, will disappear, and we will have perfect bodies for the heaven that God has prepared for us.

A woman whose husband was obliterated by a bomb in Vietnam asked me, "What about the body of my husband? What will it be like in the resurrection? It was totally destroyed!" Well, thank God, God is not dependent upon the wholeness of the human body being preserved. We are all made of dust and to dust we return. God gives us new bodies. The body of this woman's husband will still be identifiable. She will still know him. Even though the Scripture says that in heaven there is neither marrying nor giving in marriage, yet she will identify him and he her. We will have the bodies that God has created and prepared for us, which are different from, and yet maintain some continuity with, the bodies that we have here. When we say that we believe in the resurrection of the body, we are affirming that the resurrected body is the perfect instrument of the spirit to accomplish in heaven for all eternity all that God has in store for us.

I close with the words of Frederick Lawrence Knowles, who wrote:

> This body is my house—It is not I:
> Herein I sojourn till, in some far sky
> I lease a fairer dwelling, built to last
> Till all the carpentry of time is past.[1]

Because Jesus rose again from the dead and gives us his Word, we can indeed affirm, "I believe in . . . the resurrection of the body."

NOTES

1. Frederick Lawrence Knowles, "My Faith," in 1,000 Quotable Poems: An Anthology of Modern Verse, comp. Thomas Curtis Clark and Esther A. Gillespie (New York: Harper & Row, 1937), 48.

Chapter 14

EVERLASTING LIFE

"I believe in . . . the Life Everlasting."

As we near the end of our consideration of the meaning of the Apostles' Creed for modern believers, we see that the creed is quite remarkable for its simplicity.

It is equally remarkable for its succinct comprehensiveness in covering all that is at the heart of the Christian faith. The Christian faith is a religion that helps us understand the past, gives instruction on how to live in the present, and also lends insight into what lies ahead.

The three basic philosophical and theological questions of life are, Where have I come from? Why am I here? Where am I going? The faith that is succinctly stated in the Apostles' Creed has, until chapter 13, dealt with the first two questions. But the affirmation of chapter 13 ("I believe in . . . the resurrection of the body") and the affirmation of this chapter opens for us a window into the future that lets the fresh breeze of hope blow upon our souls.

Many Biblical references throw light on this affirmation. Let us look first at the nighttime encounter of Jesus with Nicodemus. In his conversation with Nicodemus, Jesus says to him, "For God so loved the world that he gave his one and only Son, that whoever believes in him shall not perish but have eternal life" (John 3:16). The King James Version uses the phrase *everlasting life* for *eternal life,* so throughout this chapter these two phrases will be used interchangeably.

Before we explore what is meant by those phrases, let us look at some other passages in the New Testament that refer to everlasting life. In 1 John 2:17 the Apostle writes, "The world and its desires pass away, but the man who does the will of God lives forever." Here John refers to eternal, or everlasting, life as life that is a continuation of something that begins in this life. He talks about this in contrast with something that will end. The world passes away, and the lust that is in it. But the person who does the will of God abides forever. In chapter 5, verse 13, of that same epistle John says, "I write these things to you who believe in the name of the Son of God so that you may know that you have eternal life." He speaks of "eternal life" not as a future possession, but a present possession, something that believers can know they have, something of which they can be assured in the present. John says that his reason for writing to believers is so that they might know and not be in doubt.

Some people do not have eternal life and do not know it. Some do not have eternal life and suspect that they do not have it. Some have eternal life and do not know that they have it. And some have eternal life and are sure of it. John's purpose in writing was that believers in the Son might know that eternal life was their current possession.

Matthew relates a conversation of Jesus with his disciples about the value of following him. Jesus tells them that anything they have to sacrifice in this life in order to be true to him is not really a sacrifice, but rather is an investment. He says, "And everyone who has left houses or brothers or sisters or father or mother or children or fields for my sake will receive a hundred times as much and will inherit eternal life. But many who are first will be last, and many who are last will be first" (Matt. 19:29–30).

So Jesus is saying that anything a believer gives up in this life for the sake of Christ and the gospel is not a sacrifice, but an investment; something that will be returned to the believer with interest. Even though you might undergo persecution because of obedience to Jesus, still, in the age to come, you will see eternal life as a rich return for the painful investment.

In John 3:36 we read, "Whoever believes in the Son has eternal life, but whoever rejects the Son will not see life, for God's wrath remains on him." Eternal life comes from believing in and obeying the Son. The alternative to experiencing eternal life is to experience the wrath of God. Eternal life is the opposite of eternal death.

Once again, Jesus in speaking to his followers says, "I tell you the truth, whoever hears my word and believes him who sent me has eternal life and will not be condemned; he has crossed over from death to life" (John 5:24). Notice the tense that Jesus uses: to say that "he has crossed over" is to speak of an action already accomplished. Eternal life has already started for those who believe. It is life that is free from impending doom: those who believe "will not be condemned." In the Bible, eternal life is described with words associated with light, joy, continuation, whereas eternal death is described with words associated with darkness, fear, judgment, and pain. (See Luke 16:19–31; Revelations 1:18, 6:8, 21:23 and 22:5.)

In the fifteenth chapter of First Corinthians, which is the touchstone chapter on the resurrection, Paul writes, "If only for this life we have hope in Christ, we are to be pitied more than all men." vs 19 Why? Ask those Christians in North Korea or China who have spent years in prison because of their faith. "Has your expectation of Christ paid off in this life?" They would have to answer no. What about those Christians down through the course of church history who have, in their obedience to Christ and their faithfulness to him, been persecuted and imprisoned, many of them paying the price of martyrdom: "Has your expectation of Christ paid off in this life?" They would have to say no. If our hope in Christ is only for what we can get out of Him during our lifetimes, we are of all people most to be pitied. If life everlasting were not the end result of following Jesus, we would all be better off adapting ourselves to the social, political, cultural, and religious climates of our communities.

Yes, there are some Christians who have enjoyed peace and prosperity. But many who have come to Christ have experienced new temptations and new conflicts that have stayed with them for their lifetimes. They do not know the joy and the peace and the ultimate reality of the gospel in this life. That will come only later.

What is everlasting life? Does eternal life mean merely going on forever? Is it just an indefinite extension of a lease? Nicodemus was a good man. He was described by John as "a member of the Jewish ruling council" (John 3:1). That means that he was a member of the Sanhedrin, and therefore, a respected, wise, and good man. But he had seen Jesus. He had heard him teach, had watched him work miracles; and he wanted to know more about this remarkable Person. So he came to Jesus at night, probably because he wanted the encounter kept secret (see John 3:1–21). He wanted privacy and the chance to talk without people asking him where he had been and what he had been doing.

Nicodemus said to Jesus, "We know that You are a good man and a teacher come from God because nobody can do these miracles that you do unless God is with him." I am sure that John did not record the entire conversation that Jesus had with Nicodemus, but instead cut through the peripheral matters and the small talk and got to the heart of the issue. Jesus replied to Nicodemus, "Nicodemus, unless a person is born again, he cannot enter the kingdom of heaven." The King James Version says "again." The Revised Standard Version says "anew." Other versions say "born from above." All of them are equally legitimate translations of the Greek word *anothen,* which means, in this context, "spiritual life that comes from God."

Nicodemus, accustomed as he was to the natural order of things, asked, "How can that be possible? Can a person enter his mother's womb a second time and be born again?"

Jesus said to him, "Nicodemus, you do not understand. I am not talking about a second physical birth, because the flesh can give life only to flesh. Everything you are can be explained naturally. You are the natural product of the union of your mother and father, and you are the intellectual and emotional product of all of the influences that have been brought to bear upon your life. Nicodemus, there is nothing about you that cannot be explained naturally. But that which is natural about you will never inherit the kingdom of God. The only way that you can get into the kingdom of God is if something supernatural happens, for the life that inherits the kingdom of God is life that is conceived by the Spirit of God. That which is born of the flesh is flesh. That which is born of the Spirit is spirit. Nicodemus, everything about you is natural." (This is an interpretive paraphrase of the conversation in John 3.)

Jesus was talking about the introduction of a spiritual quality of life, something that only God can do. It is the work of God's Spirit. So whether we call it being "born again," or being "born anew," or being "born from above," it is all the same thing. It is God's life made available in our human lives, and when it comes in, it starts now. Eternity does not wait until later to begin. That is why Jesus could say that "he who believes in me will live, even though he dies; and whoever lives and believes in me will never die" (John 11:25–26). Why? Because the life of God implanted in the human heart cannot die. That is the nature of eternal life. And eternal life is something that we must remember is a gift of God, not achieved by human effort, lest, in achieving it, we become proud of our own works.

Everlasting life is called everlasting life, or eternal life, because it is of the quality that does not end when material things pass away. It is what Jesus was talking about when he said to his disciples, "I have come that you might have life, and have it to the full" (John 10:10). Not mere existence, but a whole new dynamic that knows no limit and knows no end. It is what Paul referred to when he wrote in Galatians 2:20, "I have been crucified with Christ and I no longer live, but Christ lives in me. The life I live in the body, I live by faith in the Son of God, who loved me and gave himself for me."

Allow me to illustrate this concept of life everlasting. A spaceship from an alien planet lands on earth. The passengers on that spaceship are capable of sustaining life in this planet's atmosphere. They set up a colony of their planet. Their way of life and their interpersonal relationships reflect the life of the planet from which they have come.

That is very much what happened to the Pilgrims when they came to this country. The colonies were reflections of Old World life, alien to the Native Americans, or Indians, who lived here.

In the same way, Christian living, as reflected in personal conduct and in the corporate life of the church, means living out the anticipated quality of life that is heaven. Christians are heaven's aliens on a strange planet, living the life of eternity as taught in the Bible and modeled by Jesus Christ.

The Scripture says that everlasting life is a different quality of life. It is heaven's life introduced into the here and now. It comes through the living presence of Jesus Christ and by the power of his Spirit as he takes up residence within us.

Eternal life is not merely a hope for the future, it is a possession of the present. It shows itself in the lives of those in whom Christ dwells; they live this eternal life now. Eternal life is the life of heaven, which invades this world through the lives of people in whose hearts the Holy Spirit has implanted heaven. The church is a colony of heaven on earth; in this way the reality of heaven is reflected on earth. Every Christian is a miniature Christ; that is what it means to be a Christian. These miniature Christs live eternal life in the home, in the office, on the golf course, at the grocery store, and behind the wheel of the car.

The early Christians were so successful in living this new way of life that they were accused by the pagan world of turning the world upside down. Of course they did not turn it upside down. Sin had already made chaos of the world. Those Christians simply were trying to set it right side up. But when you are living upside down, anything right side up looks like it is upside down. Those early Christians were conscious of the immanent presence of God as revealed in Jesus Christ. They lived with a high sense of the call to holiness as exemplified in the life of their Master. Their value system was based upon the reality of heaven as opposed to the comforts, pleasures, and possessions of this world. Those early Christians were, and we, as Christians, are, called to be great lovers in the very best sense of that word. In love they were willing to invest their lives in sacrificial obedience to the gospel of Jesus Christ, and in unselfish service to one another. Those early Christians were convinced of the hope of the resurrection and of heaven, so they lived with a cheerful abandon, dedicating themselves to the One who is Life itself. They even knew that Life was worth dying for. Yes, I believe in the life everlasting.

In Peru, I understand, there was a famous admiral who was killed in a battle off of the coast of Chile. To this day, at all military reviews, the admiral's name is called. Each time, an orderly steps forward, and pointing upward, he answers, "Absent, but accounted for. He is with the heroes." This is surely the case with our departed brothers and sisters in Christ. They are absent, but accounted for with Jesus Christ, and with the heroes of the faith.

David Redding, in his delightful book, *God is Up to Something,* says, "Anyone who feels sorry for a dead Christian, as though the poor chap were missing something, is himself missing the trans-figuring promotion involved. This is what we mean by the good news."[1]

Yes, I believe in the life everlasting.

NOTES

1. David A. Redding, *God is Up to Something,* Word, Inc., 1972, p. 107.

ADDENDUM

Evaluating the Competition

We live in a world of faiths that compete with one another for the souls of people. It has always been like that. When God gave the Ten Commandments to Moses to be delivered to the Jews, the first command was a prohibition: "You shall have no other gods before me" (Exod. 20:3).

A "god" is what people trust and adore, and upon which they base their hopes. A god may be as simple as a primitive idol carved from wood before which people prostrate themselves. Or a god may be as complicated as a philosophical system based on abstractions about the ultimate ground of being.

Faith as a verb is the trust we exercise in the god of our choice. Faith as a noun is the body of belief that surrounds that god and defines our relationship to that god.

Thus, Christians have faith (verb) in God, who is revealed as Father, Son, and Holy Spirit. The Christian faith (noun) is the body of doctrine that defines who this Trinity is, how God has revealed Himself to us, what He has done for us, and what He wants us to do in response to Him.

In the New Testament there is the brief book of Jude—just one chapter long—written by Jude to some Christians to warn them about the conflicting faiths they face. He tells them,

Dear friends, although I was very eager to write to you about the salvation we share, I felt I had to write and urge you to contend for the faith that was once for all entrusted to the saints. For certain men whose condemnation was written about long ago have secretly slipped in among you. They are godless men, who change the grace of our God into a license for immortality and deny Jesus Christ our only Sovereign and Lord. (Jude 1:3–4)

Jude is aware that the true Christian faith (noun) is open to distortion, called heresy, by the very people who profess to believe it. There is danger from within the church.

But also, as Christians come in contact with other faiths, especially now in America with the tremendous influx of Asian immigrants, Christians are faced with competing ideas that conflict with true Christianity. Some of these ideas, such as Buddhism, are ancient religions. Some, like the New Age movement, are a mixture of old and new religious thought.

How do we evaluate the competition to the biblical faith of Christianity?

Evaluating religions means making value judgments. Value judgments tend to be very subjective. Two people may not agree on what constitutes good art versus bad art, but the very fact that the discussion can take place is an affirmation of the existence of opposites in value. When making such subjective judgments, it is best not to be too dogmatic.

A little boy was traveling out West with his mother, who took him to an art exhibit in Denver. They walked through the exhibition hall and looked at the displays, all of which bored the boy to tears, with the exception of one particularly abstract work. The boy looked at it and tried to figure it out. Finally, he said to his mother, "What is that supposed to be?" She went over and read the title plaque on the frame and said, "This is supposed to be a man and his horse." He stepped back a few paces, looked at the picture again from every angle, and finally asked, "Why ain't it?"

Now that kind of question tells us more about the boy's understanding of art than it tells us about the picture. Some people like traditional art and some like abstract art; it is a subjective value judgment, and it is difficult to say that a painting is good or bad just because one person happens to like it or dislike it.

I remember getting a lesson in art in 1974, shortly after going on the board of *Christianity Today, Inc.* One of the first board meetings I attended was at the O'Hare Hilton Hotel in Chicago. I was assigned to room with a wonderful Christian business executive, who has since gone to be with the Lord. His name was Maxey Jarman. He had just retired as chair of the board of Genesco. He loved the Lord, he loved the Bible. He taught the Bible. He was a very articulate and very conservative Christian.

The decor of the O'Hare Hilton was quite contemporary. The furniture and lamps had lots of chrome, and the walls were covered with metallic papers. Every room had one or more abstract paintings or drawings; the frames were of chrome or aluminum or stainless steel.

As we were unpacking our bags, I made some comment about the art, and Maxey said, "You know, that's my hobby."

"What's your hobby?" I asked. Somehow I had assumed that a man that conservative would love Rembrandt or Rubens.

He said, "My hobby is painting abstract art." Then he proceeded to tell me about abstract art. When he finished I had a new understanding for what made it art. Although my taste runs to more traditional art, I realize that my taste does not determine what is good or great art.

In matters of taste, value judgments are almost always subjective. But when it comes to function, the usefulness of an object, what is good and what is bad can be more objectively evaluated. Two people might disagree on the aesthetics of a building's design, but if the building was to collapse under the weight of its occupants, all would agree that it was a bad building. It did not function as a building should function. A bridge might be viewed as a graceful work of art by some people, and by others as a monstrosity. But if it safely handled the traffic load of the highway of which it was a part, it would be considered a good bridge. Maybe not a pretty bridge, but a good bridge. Why? It functioned as a bridge should function.

When we try to evaluate religion, we must be very careful. For one thing, much evaluation of religion or religious experience is subjective. It is a matter of taste. Some people go to a certain church because they like its formality; others go to a different church because they like its informality. That is a matter of taste.

When it comes to theology and truth, however, there is a more accurate way to judge what is good and what is bad. A person's religion is a very personal thing. It is neither in good taste nor kind to make light of what other people sincerely hold dear. We should never be flippant in judging other religions. Jesus was rough on the Pharisees, and yet individually he took them very seriously. Jesus told the Samaritan woman at the well that she was wrong and that her religion was wrong, but he did not make fun of her, nor did he make fun of her religion (John 4:1–26, especially verse 22).

The historical foundation for the Christian faith makes it, to at least some extent, verifiable. The Christian faith rises or falls on the truth of the resurrection of Jesus Christ. The gospel is true because it is rooted in what God has done. He is still at work in recreating that which he created and which we, through our sin, have so terribly marred. We are here as a result of God's deliberate creative intention. We are not here as the result of some random process. We were created to be the objects of God's love, not the objects of his wrath. We have all the potential for fellowship with our heavenly Father, and we have been made to enjoy this fellowship. That is why there is this longing within all of us to know well and to be known well by at least one other person. This longing is, at its core, a deep desire for fellowship with God.

To be saved means to be put back on the track of God's good purposes for us. To be lost means to be off the track or headed in the wrong direction.

To be saved means that we are forgiven for our sins, and we do not have to live with guilt. To be lost means that we are still guilty before the righteous God.

To be saved means to walk in the light of God's revelation and God's truth. To be lost means to be still groping in the darkness of doubt and uncertainty.

To be saved is to have the assurance that our ultimate destination is the eternal presence of God, that which the Bible calls heaven. To be lost means that our ultimate destination is eternal separation from this God of love, that which the Bible calls hell.

How do we know all of this? Because this is the gospel "once for all entrusted to the saints" to which Jude refers. As Phillips translates Jude 1:3, "I fully intend, dear friends, to write to you about our common salvation but I feel compelled to make my letter to you an earnest appeal to put up a real fight for the faith which has been once for all committed to those who belong to Christ."

Jude talks about a faith for which a fight must be fought. Why must this fight be fought? Why does a person contend for the faith? Because it is under attack. It can be distorted by those who are on the inside. And it is opposed by religions that are contrary to it.

In talking about the competition, I am not talking about other congregations or even denominations. Not at all. Any church that confesses faith in Jesus Christ as Lord and Savior should be considered friend and not foe.

The competition is false ideas, ideas about God (that is, theology) that are not true. These ideas may sneak into the church in the form of alien ideas that are foisted off on the people as some new light or new revelation. Or these ideas may be ideas that come from other religious groups that are not historically and traditionally Christian. The competition I am talking about is the competition of ideas, not people. Even though the ideas are perpetrated by people, the enemy is not people. The enemy is the idea that competes for our ultimate faith and loyalty.

When Jude talks about contending for the faith, he says specifically that there are some who change (the King James Version uses the word *pervert*) the grace of our God. Grace is God's attitude toward sinful people, which leads him to do for us what we desperately need, not what we deserve. Grace is the underlying attitude of God, by which he provides for us everything that is necessary for life and salvation. We cannot earn it. As the Apostle Paul says, "For it is by grace you have been saved, through faith—and this not from yourselves, it is the gift of God—not by works, so that no one can boast. For we are God's workmanship, created in Christ Jesus to do good works, which God prepared in advance for us to do (Eph. 2:8–10).

But some people say, "If salvation is by faith, and we cannot earn it, then let's believe in Jesus to save us and live like we please." They use grace and faith as an excuse for living in any way that they want.

Then there are others who simply cannot accept this grace. They have to add something to it. That was the struggle of the early church. It tried to propagate the Christian faith—the gospel of salvation by grace through faith alone in Jesus Christ—to those who had been steeped in the rituals, laws, and traditions of Judaism. Those early Jews who became Christians brought their Jewish rituals with them and tried to make the Gentiles become Jews first before they could become Christians. This is what the book of Galations is about.

So if we must evaluate the competition in order to defend the faith, what do we look for? What are some guidelines in spotting the wrong ideas, the contradictory theological concepts, the competing ideologies, that may come to us from outside the church? Let me suggest several.

First, always look at the source of the idea. Historic Christianity has said for centuries that the Bible is the Word of God, the only infallible rule of faith and practice. It is the Scriptures that were inspired by the Holy Spirit and recorded as an accurate instrument to teach us what God wants us to believe about Him and what duty He requires of us. When people come with a new idea that is not based upon Scripture, watch out. Ask them what the basis of their theology and of their lives is.

Also, look at the moral quality of the leadership. In verses 17–19 of the short letter of Jude, Jude warns, "But remember, beloved, the predictions of the Apostles of our Lord Jesus Christ; they said to you, 'In the last time there will be scoffers.'" Scoffers are people who make fun of that which they do not understand. "Following their own ungodly passions, they are ruled by their own lusts. It is these people who set up divisions." Here Jude is not speaking of the division that Jesus said he came to bring. He said in Matthew 10:34, "I have not come to bring peace, but a sword." Those who believe in Jesus and take him seriously and follow him will find themselves separated from some other people, even within their own families.

But Jude says that these people set up artificial divisions in that the leader may demand loyalty to himself or herself. Or the leader may demand loyalty to his or her particular interpretation of a verse of Scripture that is open to different interpretations; this type of leader insists that his or her interpretation alone is the right one, thus dividing people. Jude goes on to refer to these people as "worldly people devoid of the Spirit." So look at the moral quality of the leadership, and then ask some questions about their theology.

Assuming that they believe in the existence of God, all religions seek to answer four questions: 1) What is God like? 2) How has he revealed himself to us? 3) What has God done for us? 4) What does God expect us to do in response to him?

In evaluating any teaching of religion, ask yourself questions like these. First, how is truth to be known? What is the source of knowledge and authority in religious matters? Is it the Scriptures? Is it the historic Christian faith? Or does this teaching have some new light, some new interpretation, that is strange and foreign to what the Bible teaches us? Second, what does it teach about the nature of human beings as to the effects of sin? What is sin? What is the image of God in human beings? Are people simply imperfect and need to be perfected, or are people sinners and need saving? Is the body on the table merely a sick patient who needs proper medication, or is this a corpse that needs new life? The Scriptures say that we are dead in trespasses and sins until we know Christ. Therefore we are not simply sick people needing to be made well; we need new life and only Christ can bring that. That is what regeneration means.

Another question to ask is what is the church's mission in the world. Is it merely to make people more confortable? To improve their environment? Don't forget that the first sin was committed, not in the ghetto, but in paradise. The problem is primarily a problem of the human heart. That does not mean that we as Christians are not to be involved in helping people who are unfortunate. But the command of Jesus to take care of the needy is still very much a command that we do out of obedience to Christ, not because that is the way ultimately to change society. The only way we can change society is to put people in touch with the living Lord, who can change them from the inside out.

Another question you may want to ask people from different religious groups is for them to define their terms. What do they mean when they talk about salvation? What do they mean when they talk about Jesus Christ and God and Spirit? Are they using these words and terms in the same way that you are and that the Christian church does?

I heard several months ago about a burglar who didn't have his theology straight. This burglar broke into a house at night. As he was tiptoeing down the hallway with his flashlight he heard a voice say, "Jesus is watching you." He stopped dead in his tracks. When nothing else happened he thought it must have been his imagination, so he continued on down the hallway. Again he heard the voice, "Jesus is watching you." He stopped short, but no lights went on, nobody else appeared, and he thought that maybe it was a recording that was a part of a new burglar alarm system. He went down to the end of the hall, and as he turned the corner he shone his flashlight through a door. There in the doorway was a huge dog with a mouthful of white teeth. Not being a dumb burglar, he decided that the best thing for him to do was to retreat. So he backed down the hall, and again he heard the voice, "Jesus is watching you." As he got to the end of the hall and was turning to make his way out, his flashlight shone through a doorway and there sitting in a cage was a mynaw bird. As his light fell on the bird, the bird said, "Jesus is watching you." The burglar breathed a sigh of relief, and said, "You dumb bird. Is that all you can say?" And then the bird said, "Sic 'em, Jesus."

You see, if that burglar had better understood theology, he would have known that not everybody who uses the name Jesus is speaking about the same person.

In religious matters it is important when we are talking to those whom we think may represent the competition to make sure that we understand the terms they are using and whether they are using them in the biblical historic sense or are talking about another Jesus.

How are we to be saved? Are we saved by performing certain works? Or going through certain rituals? Or by loyalty to a leader? (Remember Jim Jones in Guyana.) Or are we saved by grace through faith alone? And what are the teachings about the church? What is the nature of the people of God and the Body of Christ? What about human responsibility? Are we called to holiness and righteousness and obedience, or is life merely a matter of achieving our own goals without regard for others?

There is competition out there for our minds and hearts and souls. Jude warns us to be alert to competing ideologies that would like to lure us away from that One who is the truth, the way, and the life itself. And he closes with beautiful praise to God almighty: "To him who is able to keep you from falling and to present you before his glorious presence without fault and with great joy—to the only God our Savior be glory, majesty, power and authority, through Jesus Christ our Lord, before all ages, now and forevermore! Amen" (Jude 24 and 25).

What a magnificent reassurance that is. In this cosmic struggle between God and Satan, between good and evil, between light and darkness, in which you and I are the front lines, we belong to the One who is able to keep us from falling and to present us without blemish before the presence of God.

It is to Him that all glory and praise and honor are due now and forever.